LO

NATURE CRAFTS

FOR

CHRISTMAS

NATURE CRAFTS

FOR

CHRISTMAS

A Step-by-Step Guide to Making Wreaths, Ornaments & Decorations

DAWN CUSICK & CAROL TAYLOR

OUR MISSION

We publish books that empower people's lives.

RODALE ❧ BOOKS

If you have any questions or comments concerning this book, please write to:
Rodale Press, Inc.
Book Readers' Service
33 East Minor Street
Emmaus, PA 18098

Printed in the United States of America on acid-free ∞, recycled ♲ paper, containing 10 percent post-consumer waste

Published by Rodale Press, Inc.
33 East Minor Street, Emmaus, PA 18098

Rodale Press Staff:
      Executive Editor: Margaret Lydic Balitas
      Editor: Cheryl Winters Tetreau
      Horticultural Consultant: Nancy J. Ondra
      Copy Editor: Nancy Bailey
      Book Designer: Patricia Field

Created and produced by Altamont Press, Inc.
50 College Street, Asheville, NC 28801

Altamont Press Staff:
      Art Director: Kathleen Holmes
      Production: Elaine Thompson and Kathleen Holmes
      Photography: Evan Bracken (unless otherwise noted)
      Illustrations: Orrin Lundgren
      Cover Photography: Richard Baab
      Cover Art Director: Dana Irwin
      Cover Stylist: Jodi Matthews

The editors at Rodale Press hope you will join with us in preserving nature's beauty so that others may share in the enjoyment of nature crafting. Unless you are certain that the plants or plant materials you are collecting—including leaves, stems, bark, flowers, fruits, seeds, or roots—are very common in your area or over a wide geographic area, please do not collect them. And do not disturb or collect any plants or plant materials from parks, natural areas, or private lands without the permission of the owner.

To the best of our knowledge, the plants and plant materials recommended in this book are common natural materials that can be grown and collected without harm to the environment.

Library of Congress Cataloging-in-Publication Data

Cusick, Dawn.
    Nature crafts for Christmas : a step-by-step guide to making wreaths, ornaments
& decorations / by Dawn Cusick & Carol Taylor.
      p. cm.
    Includes bibliographical references and index.
    ISBN 0–87596–622–5 hardcover
    1. Christmas decorations. 2. Nature craft. I. Taylor, Carol. II. Title.
TT900.C4C855 1994
745.594'12—dc20   94–15975
                                                     CIP

Distributed in the book trade by St. Martin's Press

2 4 6 8 10 9 7 5 3 1 hardcover

CONTENTS

CONTRIBUTORS 10

WE WISH YOU A MERRY CHRISTMAS! 12

SANTA'S WORKSHOP:
BASIC CRAFT TOOLS AND TECHNIQUES 14

THE PROJECTS 32

WELCOME, CHRISTMAS! 34

DECK THE HALLS 80

OH CHRISTMAS TREE! 148

THE CHRISTMAS TABLE 222

MAIL-ORDER SOURCES 252

BIBLIOGRAPHY 252

INDEX 253

CONTRIBUTORS

Craft Design

Crystal Allen is a graphic designer and watercolorist living in the Blue Ridge Mountains. Crystal gardens extensively and enjoys creating projects with natural materials. (page 84)

Nora Blose is a frequent contributor to craft books and coauthor of *The Herb Drying Handbook* (Sterling Publishing, 1992). She markets her herbal crafts under the name Nora's Follies and frequently shares her love of herbs with garden clubs and school groups. Nora takes great pleasure in crafting with friends, and the projects featured here were created with Michelle West. (pages 106 and 116)

Julianne Bronder has enjoyed creating floral designs for numerous craft books and publications, in addition to work she's done for her own shop and for a wholesale design house. Julianne graduated from the American Floral Art School in Chicago, Illinois, and currently resides in Westmont, Illinois. (pages 43–45, 51, 87, 92, 113, 115, 126, 128, 143, 146, 153, 171, 200, 201, 207, 208, 214, 226, 232, and 237)

Darlene Conti is a floral designer and nature crafter living in western North Carolina. She especially enjoys working with fragrant materials. (page 203)

Alice Ensley enjoys dabbling in a wide variety of crafts, from nature crafts to sewing, as well as experimenting with new materials. Many of her crafts are modern versions of traditional Appalachian crafts she remembers from her childhood. Alice lives in Candler, North Carolina, with her husband and five children. (pages 64, 65, 160, and 221)

Judith Fox creates her cornhusk crafts for a variety of national and international clients. She lives in Morristown, Tennessee, where she grows herbs and flowers for her business, Willow Hill Farm, and teaches craft workshops. (page 164)

Janet Frye is the proprietor of the Enchanted Florist, a floral design shop in Arden, North Carolina. She works primarily with natural materials and specializes in designing projects that showcase the natural shapes, textures, and colors of the materials. Janet often collaborates with coworker Beth Hohensee. (pages 234, 236, and 250)

Fred Tyson Gaylor is a product designer for Hanford's, a wholesale holiday accessory company in Charlotte, North Carolina. Fred's job requires a great deal of national and international travel, and he enjoys watching the development of material and style trends. (page 97)

Cynthia Gillooly and **Jamie McCabe** enjoy creating natural designs from unusual materials. Cynthia owns the Golden Cricket, a floral design studio in Asheville, North Carolina, where she also teaches floral design classes. Cynthia and Jamie have worked together for several years, and together they have more than 25 years of experience. (pages 38, 58, 72, 76, 152, 245, and 247)

Jeannette Hafner grows the majority of her craft herbs and flowers in her gardens in Orange, Connecticut. She markets her wreaths, arrangements, and small gift items at craft fairs and also teaches drying and design techniques. Her floral and herbal crafts have been featured in numerous craft books and publications. (pages 83, 107, 110–111, 125, 135, 170, 229, 239, and 249)

Clodine Hamilton has won several first-place awards at the world's largest gourd show, held annually in Mount Gilead, Ohio. She grows her gourds on the latticework around her garage and enjoys creating individual identities for each figure, often painting five or six at a time. Clodine sells her painted gourds from her home in Mishawaka, Indiana, and uses word-of-mouth recommendations as her only advertising. (pages 54, 55, 89, 102, 103, 130, 131, 185, 187, 191, and 193-left)

Judy Mofield Mallow's family boasts five generations of basket makers. She specializes in art baskets and assorted crafts made from pine needles and has recently begun experimenting with baskets made with a combination of carved gourds and pine needles. She markets her work under the name of Prim Pines in Carthage, North Carolina. (pages 49, 141, 150, 151, 156, 157, 159, 174, 177, 182, 197, 206, 209, and 216)

Janie Markley teaches science at the middle school level and enjoys crafts as a way to wind down at the end of hectic days. Many of her crafts are variations of the crafts her family collected from previous generations. She lives in the mountains of western North Carolina with her husband and two children. (pages 196 and 219)

Kit Meckley has always loved collecting interesting natural materials. Several years ago, after taking a few classes from a floral designer and apprenticing in a design shop, she began making crafts with her collected materials. Her projects are always inspired from her collections, and she especially enjoys cones. Kit also likes collecting and working with weeds and grasses. (pages 60, 68, 77, and 241)

Alyce Nadeau grows more than 200 varieties of herbs for her herbal craft business, Goldenrod Mountain Herbs, in Deep Gap, North Carolina. Alyce's most recent craft adventures include creating new herbal vinegar recipes and drying natural materials in the microwave. Her first book, a guide to starting a small herb business, will be available in 1995. (pages 37, 95, 100, 109, 120, 137, 139, 167, 169, 172, 188, 189, 204, 213, 215, 225, 227, and 243)

Mary Wojeck is a gourd crafter from Traveller's Rest, South Carolina. Although she enjoys many crafts, her favorite pastime is creating and painting fanciful animals from gourds. Mary's gourds have been on display in several national science museums. (pages 121, 190, and 193-right)

Additional Photography

Tim Barnwell: pages 34–35.

T. L. Gettings/Rodale Stock Images: pages 32–33.

Bill Lea: pages 7–9.

Mitch Mandel/Rodale Stock Images: pages 222–223.

Alison Miksch/Rodale Stock Images: pages 14–15.

Rodale Stock Images: pages 12–13, 148–149.

Also thanks to the people who contributed locations and props:

Peter and Lorna Sterling, Porker's Rest, Clyde, North Carolina; Sherri and Eric Allen, Canton, North Carolina; Carla and Marc SanAntonio, Clyde, North Carolina; Richmond Hill Bed and Breakfast, Asheville, North Carolina; handmade chairmaker Mark Taylor, Asheville, North Carolina; Juanita Metcalf of Juan's Quilt Cabin, Clyde, North Carolina; Deborah Henderson of Sweets and Feasts, Asheville, North Carolina; Kandi and Steve King of Mountain View Nursery, Clyde, North Carolina; and Alyce Nadeau of Goldenrod Mountain Herbs, Deep Gap, North Carolina.

WE WISH YOU A MERRY CHRISTMAS!

Something about this season makes us long for a home filled to the rafters with fresh-picked evergreens, hand-tied ribbons, and homemade decorations of every sort. If you're an experienced crafter, you know that decking the halls with your own handmade ornaments is one of the best parts of Christmas.
If you're a novice who's never made so much as a pine swag before, your first home-crafted Christmas can be a memorable one.

The materials you'll be working with are certainly beautiful. Evergreens come in an astonishing array of colors, all different, all called green. Pinecones are complex studies in geometric precision. Brilliant red berries, gleaming gold ribbon, willowy pine needles, knobby-shelled walnuts—creating something ugly out of these materials is difficult. And nothing about nature crafts is daunting—we'll take you step-by-step through the making of each craft in this book. The result will be a beautiful holiday craft you'll be proud to display or give as a gift. Our fondest wish is that, whether you're a beginner or an old hand, you'll find something in the following pages for every room in your house or for every person on your gift list.

Of course, we invite you to ignore us. You know your own tastes and preferences and those of your family. If our instructions call for 15 dried red roses and you don't have any dried red roses or you don't like dried red roses, we urge you to substitute something that's available to you and that you like better.

The test of a successful project is straightforward: Does it please you? If it does, the chances are that it will also please your family and friends. So make the most of your holiday season by making most of these crafts—we're sure you won't be disappointed.

Happy Holidays!

Santa's Workshop: Basic Craft Tools and Techniques

The tools for nature crafts are as common as wildflowers, as unpretentious as wild grasses, and if not as free as pinecones on the forest floor, then as inexpensive as gourds at the farmers' market. The techniques for nature crafts are as useful as garden herbs and as adaptable as wild grapevines.

Because of their versatile simplicity, the tools and techniques leave the crafter enormous scope in selecting which natural materials to use and in deciding how to put them together.

❧ SELECTING TOOLS ❧

All the essential tools for nature crafts are either already lying around your house or waiting at the craft store or discount mart. Here's a rundown.

Culinary Wreath, see page 238

Floral Picks

An everyday tool of professional florists for decades, floral picks have been discovered by home crafters who work with flowers, greenery, and other materials as well. Floral picks are short, thin, matchsticklike pieces of wood with one pointed end and one blunt end. Attached to the blunt end is a length of fine-gauge wire.

Floral picks allow you to attach flimsy or bulky materials to a base. While a strong-stemmed pine branch can be inserted directly into a block of floral foam or into a straw wreath base, a weak-stemmed lavender bloom cannot. A pick provides the necessary rigidity.

To use a floral pick, place it against the stem of the flower so that the pick extends about 1 inch below the stem. Wrap the wire around the stem and the pick once or twice, then spiral the wire down the length of the pick, binding the pick and the stem together. If the stems are especially delicate, you can add extra strength by wrapping the picked stems with floral tape.

An especially time-saving technique is to make mini bouquets. Group the materials into small bouquets of three to five stems and attach all the stems of each group to one pick (see Figure 1). The bouquets can then be picked into the base, allowing for much faster coverage than a stem-by-stem application. Any material with a long, thin shape—a cinnamon stick, for example—can be wired to a floral pick.

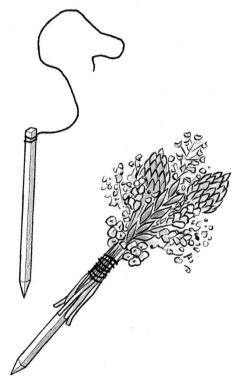

Figure 1

With materials that are not conveniently elongated, however, it is often easier to pull the wire off the pick and hot-glue the item to the pick. When you're working with fruits and vegetables, a good strategy is to remove the pick's wire, insert the sharp end of the pick into the fruit, then wire or hot-glue the blunt end of the pick to the base. In fact, crafters have found so many uses for floral picks that craft picks are now available with no wires attached. If you plan to attach a lot of non-floral materials, the easiest thing to do is simply buy the unwired picks.

Floral Pins

These U-shaped pieces of sturdy wire resemble old-fashioned hairpins and work much the same way. To use a floral pin, simply place the materials you're attaching against a straw or foam base, position the pin with its prongs on either side of the materials, and press the pin into the base at an angle (see Figure 2).

Pinecone Bird Nest, see page 150

wire—for example, making a wreath base by covering a metal ring with artemisia—spool wire is extremely convenient. To cut floral wire to the exact length required, you'll need wire cutters or heavy-duty scissors.

To strengthen a single stem with floral wire, place a length of wire against the stem so that the two overlap as much as possible. Then wrap floral tape around them both, spiraling down the stems at an angle and stretching the tape as you wrap (see Figure 3).

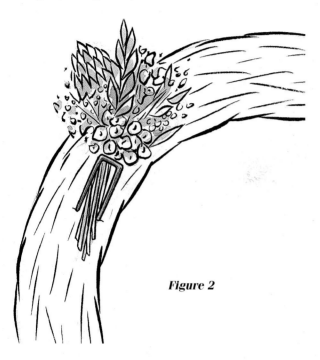

Figure 2

Floral Tape

For many purposes, the crafter can use just about any strong, durable tape. Electrical tape, for example, will do a fine job of securing a block of floral foam to a saucer or shallow bowl, creating a base for an arrangement. For most other purposes, floral tape is superior.

Available in green or brown to blend with natural materials, floral tape is not sticky to the touch. Rather, to make it adhere, you must stretch it as you wrap. In combination with floral wire, it can be used to strengthen a single stem (see "Floral Wire" below), or it can be wrapped around several stems, thus creating a large bouquet to insert in a nosegay holder.

Floral Wire

Floral wire comes in a variety of thicknesses, or "gauges," ranging from very thin and pliable (fine-gauge floral wire) to very thick and sturdy (heavy-gauge floral wire). You can purchase floral wire on a continuous spool or precut into various lengths. For a project requiring a fair amount of

Figure 3

Frequently, the most efficient way to attach an item to a wreath, arrangement, or ornament is to wire it on. Wiring is especially useful on wreaths because the base is a convenient diameter for wrapping wire around. Grapevine bases are perfect; each coil of vine provides a point of purchase.

To wire an object, first look for an inconspicuous place to attach the wire. If there is none, plan to conceal the wire later with other materials such as flowers and foliage.

Since pinecones are among the most commonly wired objects, they provide a ready example. Using wire cutters or heavy-duty scissors, cut a 12-inch length of fine-gauge floral wire. (The actual length will vary with the size of the cone and the size of the object you are wiring it to.) Fold the wire loosely in half and slip it around the cone between two layers of "petals" near the bottom of the cone. Twist the wire ends together right next to the cone. Hold the cone tightly against the wreath base with the wire ends straddling the base, and again twist the wire ends until the cone is held firmly in place (see Figure 4).

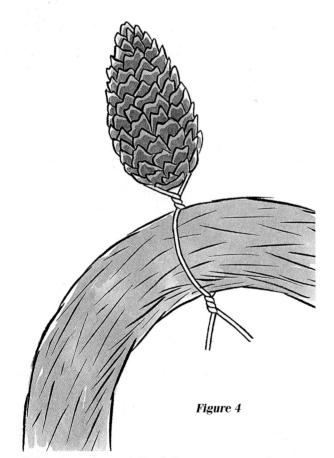

Figure 4

If the cone is especially delicate, you may fare better if you carefully loop the end of the wire around it, leaving yourself a single long stem to wrap around or insert into the base (see Figure 5).

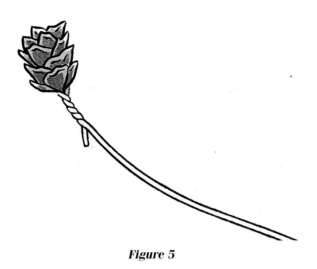

Figure 5

A distant (and undervalued) relative of floral wire is monofilament fishing line, available in department stores, many hardware stores, and sporting goods stores. It is remarkably flexible, practically invisible, and virtually unbreakable. Its disadvantage is that its ends can't be simply twisted together to finish off the attachment but have to be hot-glued to the base or tied into fairly large and obnoxious knots. On certain projects with lots of concealing materials, however, monofilament fishing line is invaluable.

Glue Guns

What the microchip was to home computing, the glue gun is to home crafting—the essential technology that made it all possible. Fast, easy to use, and incredibly versatile, a glue gun allows you to affix almost anything to almost anything else.

In the last few years a cool-glue gun has appeared on the market. It uses special glue sticks that melt at a considerably lower temperature, a characteristic that has two advantages. First, you won't inflict the small but painful burns on your hands and arms that even professional florists consider inevitable with hot glue. Second, cool glue doesn't dissolve polystyrene or floral foam, which the hot glue does with discouraging regularity. The disadvantages of the cool-glue guns are also two: They are less widely available, and they require special glue sticks that are more expensive than the hot-glue kind.

White Craft Glue

Universally available, white craft glue is sold under a variety of brand names and in formulas that vary slightly. Check the label to be sure the glue will work with the materials you are using.

❧ MAKING BASES ❧

Some bases, especially wreath bases, are widely available at craft stores and discount marts. Any store with a sizable craft section will carry inexpensive foam, wire, and straw wreath bases as well as foam blocks, sheets, balls, and cones.

On the other hand, wreaths don't just come in round. Occasionally, you'll want a square base, an oval one, or a unique shape for a one-of-a-kind wreath. Creating your own bases to suit your own designs is simple and fast.

Foam Bases

A serrated knife cuts through foam with ease and turns the large blocks of foam sold in craft stores into just about any shape a crafter can think up. You can also adapt preshaped forms to your needs—for example, by cutting a foam wreath base in half to make a base for a semi-circular garland or by cutting a foam ball in half to create a base for a topiary.

Vine and Twig Bases

Unlike foam, grapevines and twigs are themselves attractive natural materials, which means that you don't have to conceal every inch of them in your finished project. Rather, they can serve as part of the overall design. Grapevine and twig bases are good choices when you're not quite sure whether you have enough natural materials to cover a base completely.

Guest Room Decorations, see page 112

Twig Wreath, see page 42

it together (see Figure 6). If fresh-cut grapevines aren't available, you can soak older vines in a tub of warm water until they soften.

To make a twig base, collect five or six dozen twigs, preferably ones that are branched and curved on their narrow ends. Form the twigs into 15 bundles, securing their wide ends with rubber bands. Using a single-wire wreath base, attach the twig bundles to the wire frame by holding a bundle parallel to the frame and wrapping fine-gauge floral wire around the bottom of the bundle and the frame (see Figure 7). Lay a second bundle so that its top overlaps the bottom of the first, hiding the rubber band, and secure it with floral wire. Continue around the wreath base until it is completely covered.

To make a curved base for a swag, simply gather several stems of twigs or grapevines together and wire them together securely in the center with medium- or heavy-gauge floral wire.

To make a grapevine wreath base, coil four to six fresh-cut grapevines into a circle, allowing them to overlap by about 2 inches. Weave one or two thin, very flexible vines around the base to hold

Figure 7

Wire Bases

Wire wreath bases are widely available in two forms. The single-wire base (also known as a crimped-wire ring) is a circle of heavy-gauge wire. The double-wire base consists of several concentric circles of wire and a series of cross wires holding them together (see Figure 8).

The single-wire base is the simplest to make yourself. Just shape any piece of heavy-gauge wire—an untwisted coat hanger will do—into a circle and wrap the two ends together with medium-gauge floral wire.

Figure 6

Double-wire bases are more complicated to repli-
cate. Considering their wide availability and low
price, they're rarely worth making yourself.

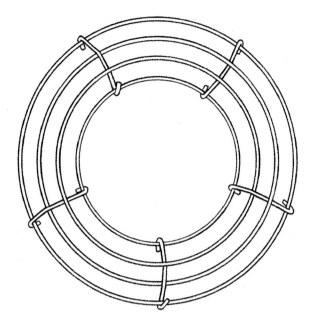

Figure 8

Figure 9

Straw Bases

Used almost exclusively for wreaths, straw bases
are especially useful if you want a full-looking
wreath and you have a lot of dried materials with
stems at least 3 inches long. To make a straw
base, hold a small handful of straw against a
single-wire base and secure the straw by wrapping fine-gauge floral wire around it and the base
at 2-inch intervals (see Figure 9). Continue
adding handfuls of straw until the wire base is
completely covered. Wrap the fine-gauge wire
around the ending point three times to secure it,
then cut the wire.

Herbal Bases

If you have an abundance of a pliable and attractive herb, you can make a base from it. The most
common choice is artemisia, whose extravagant
growth habits and attractive silver foliage make it
a popular choice. To make an artemisia base, take
a handful of the herb and hold it against a single-
wire base. Then, using either monofilament fishing line or spool wire, wrap the foliage to the
ring, wrapping every inch or so (see Figure 10).
When the handful of artemisia is secured, add a
second handful, attaching it in the same way.
Continue around the ring until it is completely

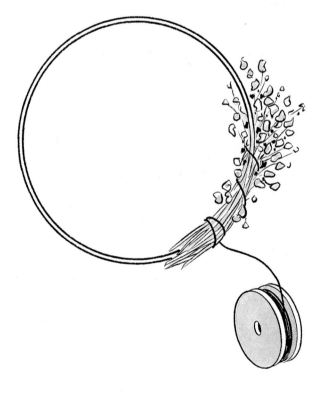

Figure 10

covered with tightly wrapped artemisia and
you have a wreath base with sides that are
about 1 inch thick.

❧ Making Hangers ❧

Almost by definition, wreaths have an empty space in the center. Thus, most of them can be hung over a nail, the knob on a cabinet door, or some other projection with no further effort on your part. Similarly, many garlands lie contentedly across a mantle or over a doorway and require no further means of support.

On the other hand, some wreaths, garlands, and swags require hangers. Fortunately, hangers require about 10 seconds and 10 inches of medium-gauge floral wire to construct.

The goal is to form a loop out of the wire and to attach that loop to the item to be hung. Many crafters prefer to wrap the wire first with floral tape to give the back a finished appearance and to protect the wall or door from possible scratches.

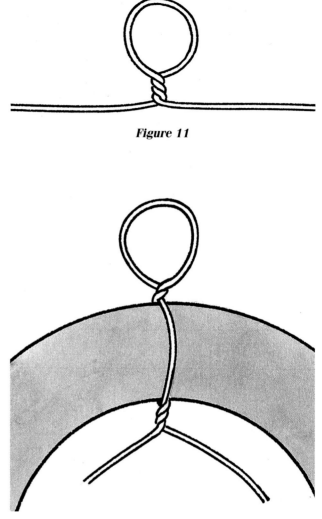

Figure 11

Figure 12

Birdseed Ornaments, see page 64

To make a hanger for a wreath, just form a loop in the center of the wire by twisting it together (see Figure 11). Then wrap the wire around the wreath base and twist the wire ends together, thus securing the hanger to the base (see Figure 12). The same technique will work for any project

with a narrow, horizontal center, such as a horizonal swag, and for most garlands, which will, of course, require several hangers depending upon how you decide to drape them. If you want your garland to drape in several curves, you'll need a hanger at the peak between every two curves (see Figure 13).

Figure 13

Magnolia Swag, see page 143

Many nonvertical swags are held together by a piece of foam; the stems of the natural materials are inserted into the foam and the foam is hung on the wall. To make a hanger for a foam-backed swag, create a loop from a 6-inch length of floral wire by twisting the ends together and trimming the excess wire (see Figure 15). Pierce the foam with the end of the hanger, positioning the hole where you want the hanger to be. Remove the hanger from the foam, place a dab of hot glue on the end of the hanger, and reinsert it into the foam. For added security, position a floral pin with its prongs on either side of the hanger, and press the pin into the base (see Figure 16). If you know the swag is especially heavy, repeat the process with a second floral pin.

Making a hanger for a vertical swag can be done while you construct the swag itself. As you wire the stems of the flowers or foliage together with medium-gauge floral wire, leave an extra 10 inches or so of wire. Form the extra wire into a loop, twist the wire end around the wire close to the stems, and trim the excess wire ends with wire cutters (see Figure 14).

Figure 15

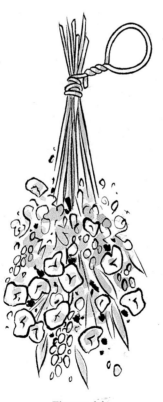

Figure 14

Figure 16

❧ MAKING WREATHS ❧

A wreath is primarily a good excuse to hang a collection of attractive materials on the wall. Often the nature and amounts of the materials you have on hand will suggest the design of the wreath. If you have a bushel of evergreens and a pint of pinecones, for example, you probably won't choose to make an elaborate cone wreath adorned with a sprig or two of Fraser fir. Even if you're collecting materials from scratch by browsing through the "dried" section of a craft store, chances are that one particular material will catch your eye and capture your heart. And once you've decided that you can't live without those exotic-looking lotus pods, lots of other design decisions have been made for you.

Attaching Background Materials

As their first layer, most wreaths have a background material of something that's abundant, relatively subdued, and easy to attach—bay leaves, artemisia, sweet Annie, or evergreens, for example. Since attaching that material stem by stem would get the wreath finished about a year later, it's usually attached in mini bouquets—small bunches of material attached to floral picks or taped together with floral tape.

Unless you're aiming for a specific effect, bouquets should be picked into foam, straw, and vine bases at the same angle, creating a clear circular line around the base. As you encircle the wreath, overlap the picks so that the foliage of each pick covers the base of the previous one. The stems from the last bouquet should be tucked neatly under the foliage of the first bouquet to make the starting and ending points indistinguishable.

With foam and straw bases, it's helpful to work in three separate stages, first covering the inner edge of the base, then the rim, then the center surface area. If you're working on a vine base, apply a dab of hot glue to the end of the pick before inserting it, for added stability.

Mini bouquets are often attached to wire bases, even herb-wrapped wire bases, with spool wire or monofilament fishing line. Rather than picking a bouquet, position it against the base and wrap spool wire several times around the stems and the base (see Figure 17). Place the bouquets so that each one covers the stems of the previous one,

Red and White Floral Wreath, see page 124

tucking the stems of the last bouquet under the foliage of the first. For a full look, alternate the direction of the foliage so that some points to the outside of the wreath, some to the inside, and some straight up the center.

Figure 17

Attaching Accent Materials

Single blooms, small sprigs of decorative foliage, and knickknacks can all be attached to the background material with hot glue or a floral pick (see Figure 18). Accent materials should appear in some predetermined pattern, either distributed evenly around the wreath or grouped together in an obviously deliberate scheme. The positioning should look as if the designer had something in mind.

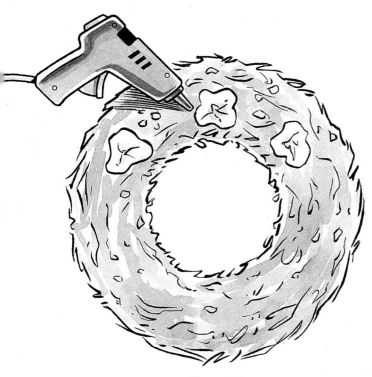

Figure 18

❧ MAKING GARLANDS ❧

A garland is long and thin, designed to drape over mantle or mirror, window or door. Making one is a matter of attaching materials to a long "spine"—anything strong enough to support the materials and flexible enough to bend and curve where you want it to. Jute cord, the kind used in macrame, makes a splendidly tough and pliable spine. Heavy-gauge floral wire also works well.

The first step in making a garland is deciding where it's going to go. Once you know that, you can measure how long it needs to be: the length of the spinet piano plus 10 inches to drape down each side, for example, or the total distance up one side of a doorway, across the top, and down the other side. If you want the garland to drape in graceful curves, make it twice as long as the banister or mantle that will support it. Once you have determined the finished length, cut the spine 12 inches longer to allow plenty of room to tie off each end after all the materials are attached.

Most crafters just lay the spine on a table or on the floor and work there. Others tie the spine between two chair backs at a convenient working height.

To make the garland, form a small bunch of foliage or flowers—six to eight stems, all going in the same direction—and wire the stems together with fine-gauge floral wire. Make a number of bunches. Then wire the bunches to the spine with the fine-gauge floral wire (see Figure 19). Make sure the leaves or flowers of each bunch overlap the stems of the previous one, concealing the wired stems and creating a full look. Continue wiring bunches to the spine until it's covered.

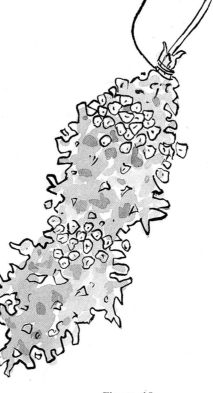

Figure 19

Before you start the actual wiring, decide how you want the bunches to lie; their direction should be deliberate rather than haphazard. One option is to work from one end of the garland to the other with the bunches all pointing in the same direction. A second possibility is to work from the center outward with the bunches on each side pointing outward. A bow, knickknack, or very full bunch of greenery or flowers can be wired or hot-glued to the center to cover the resulting bare spot.

Bunches can be composed of a single material (boxwood, for example) and alternated with bunches of other materials (pine needles and baby's-breath, for example). Alternatively, each bunch can consist of several materials.

After the spine is covered, decorative accents can be wired or hot-glued to the foliage; use pinecones, berries, knickknacks, or whatever looks like Christmas. Ribbon is especially attractive when trailed down the length of the garland with a bow wired to the center or bows wired at each end.

Figure 20

Figure 21

❊ MAKING SWAGS ❊

Broadly defined, swags are bouquets designed to hang—on a wall, a door, a cabinet, or even a lamppost. The usual (and the simplest) swag is a grouping of greenery, flowers, or even garlic bulbs wired together by their stems (see Figure 20). A bow or some other decorative accent is added to conceal the wiring.

Somewhat more complicated are horizontal swags. To make the most common type, divide the background material—'Silver King' artemisia, for example—into two bunches and place them end to end, with the stems overlapping in the center (see Figure 21). After you wire their stems together with medium-gauge floral wire, you can add additional materials with wire or hot glue. A bow or other accent wired to the center of the swag conceals the means of attachment.

A third type of swag uses a found object for a base—a craft horn, for example, or a cinnamon broom. Wire or hot-glue flowers and foliage to the object and hang your creation on the wall.

WORKING WITH FLOWERS AND HERBS

Even in the dead of winter, flowers and herbs can add wonderful colors, textures, and fragrances to the Christmas decorations that grace your home.

Fresh flowers and foliage can be used with "wet" floral foam, a fine-grained foam that absorbs and holds water. To use it, float it in a sinkful of water and allow it to hydrate at its own rate. Don't forcibly submerge it or air pockets will form in the foam—small pockets of drought for any hapless plants whose stems end up in them. Watered daily, wet foam will preserve cut flowers and greenery almost as effectively as a vase full of water.

Also available is a fine-grained floral foam designed for dry materials. Far finer in texture

Drying Flowers & Herbs

The chart below provides you with information for drying many of the most popular flowers and herbs used in crafts.

PLANT MATERIAL	DRYING METHOD
Baby's-Breath	Air-dry by hanging in small, loose bundles.
Bee Balm	Air-dry on a rack or hang upside down. Harvest the blooms early in the blooming cycle.
Blue Sage	Air-dry by hanging upside down. Handle gently to prevent damage.
Calendula	Air-dry the blooms on a drying rack or microwave them between two paper towels on low power for 1 to 3 minutes.
Caspia	Air-dry the blooms by hanging upside down in small bundles.
Chives	Air-dry the individual blooms on a rack.
Cockscomb	Air-dry by hanging upside down after foliage has been removed. Harvest early in the morning to prevent matting.
Coneflower	Air-dry on a drying rack or hang upside down in small, loose bundles.
Dusty Miller	Air-dry the foliage on a drying rack.
Feverfew	Air-dry by hanging in small, loose bundles.
Globe Amaranth	Air-dry the blooms on a drying rack.
Hydrangea	Air-dry by hanging in small, loose bundles.
Lamb's-Ears	Separate the foliage from the stems and air-dry on a drying rack. The leaves also dry well in the microwave between two paper towels on low power for 1 to 3 minutes.
Larkspur	Air-dry by hanging upside down. Harvest when most of the flowers on a stalk have opened.
Lemon Verbena	Air-dry the foliage in small, loose bundles. If curves are desired, shape the fresh-cut stems around a mold and allow to air-dry, then remove gently.
Love-in-a-Mist	Air-dry by hanging upside down. Harvest the seed heads before the first frost.
Marigolds	Air-dry the blooms on a drying rack or microwave them between two paper towels on low power for 1 to 3 minutes.
Mint	Air-dry by hanging in small, loose bundles, or air-dry the individual leaves on a rack, turning frequently if curled leaves are not desired.
Oregano	Trim the stems into 5- to 7-inch lengths and air-dry them by hanging in small, loose bundles.
Rose	Air-dry by hanging or dry in a desiccant. Harvest before the blooms are fully opened.
Sage	Cut the stems down to 3-inch lengths and air-dry them on a rack.
'Silver King' Artemisia	Air-dry by hanging if straight lines are desired; air-dry by standing upright in a vase if curved lines are desired.
Statice	Air-dry by hanging upside down.
Strawflower	Air-dry on a drying rack or by hanging upside down.
Sweet Annie	Air-dry by hanging in small, loose bundles.
Yarrow	Air-dry on a drying rack or by hanging upside down in small, loose bundles.

than polystyrene foam, brown floral foam is easier to pierce with a plant stem or even with a pick, which allows you to be gentler with delicate materials.

Dried flowers and herbs allow you to create craft projects that will last for years. A marvelous array of flowers and herbs is available at craft stores.

Even more satisfying are dried flowers and herbs from last summer's garden. If you have any available, use them for Christmas ornaments. If you don't, consider drying some next summer.

Moss Tree, see page 107

Drying flowers and herbs is astonishingly simple. To begin, harvest a good selection of materials. Do your cutting on a sunny day, after the morning dew has dried and well after any rain shower. As you select materials, keep in mind that they don't magically improve with age: Insect damage and brown spots will be even more noticeable on your front door wreath than in your garden. Pick only unblemished plants. Also, remember that most materials shrink as they dry.

Almost any plant can be dried with one of two air-drying techniques. First, you can group several stems of the same flower or herb together, secure their stems with raffia or a rubber band, and hang them upside down in a dark, dry location. A second means of air-drying—screen or rack drying—involves spreading single blooms or leaves on a wire screen so that air can circulate around the blooms on all sides. Drying times will vary depending on the type of plant and its moisture content when it was harvested. The typical range is 5 to 15 days.

A popular flower-drying method involves silica gel, a white, powdery substance available in craft stores and discount marts with large craft sections. Known as a desiccant, silica gel is a highly effective moisture absorber. To use it, alternate layers of blooms with layers of silica in a container, cover the container, and set aside. Check the progress of your blooms every few days; if allowed to overdry, they will lose some of their color. Avoid leaving dried blooms in a moist area; they will obligingly reabsorb the moisture you carefully removed.

❦ DRYING FRUIT ❦

While dried apple and orange slices are available at most craft stores, it's easy and convenient to dry your own.

Start with fresh, high-quality fruit; nothing ever comes through the drying process looking better than when it went in. If the fresh fruit has bruises or discolorations, the blemishes will be even more visible on the dried slices.

If you're drying apples, you can either remove the core or leave it intact, depending on your preferences and your project. Sprinkle apple slices with lemon juice to reduce discoloration.

Slice apples and oranges ⅛ to ¼ inch thick. Discard the end pieces and dry the remaining slices by one of the following methods.

Oven

Arrange apple or orange slices on a cookie sheet covered with waxed paper and place them in the oven at 175°F. If you have an oven thermometer, it would be wise to check the accuracy of your oven's temperature gauge; a too-hot oven will bake the fruit rather than dry it. Leave the oven door open slightly throughout the process and turn the slices once.

Drying times vary widely—from 3 to 10 hours—depending on the moisture content of the fruit and the amount you're drying at one time. Check frequently. For best results, remove the slices before they're completely dry and place them on a rack in a warm, dry place to finish drying.

Microwave

Place apple or orange slices on three layers of paper towels. Cover them with two more layers of towels and place them in the microwave. Since microwaves vary in wattage, precise times are impossible to specify. As a rule of thumb, microwave four apple or orange slices at 50 percent power for 8 minutes. Turn the slices halfway through the process, placing them on a dry portion of paper towel. Watch them carefully for burning, which will start in the center of the slice.

Food Dehydrator

Basically, follow the manufacturer's instructions. If you lost them long ago, a good rule of thumb is to dry the fruit slices for 6 hours at the high setting.

❦ Using Gourds ❦

Gourds are among our oldest and most useful domesticated plants. Lightweight, waterproof, and willing to grow in a variety of climates, gourds have been hollowed out and used as everything from sake bottles to fishing floats, from seed containers to musical instruments.

Although gourds are increasingly available at flea markets, farmers' markets, and roadside vegetable stands, many crafters enjoy growing their own. Most use some form of *Lagenaria,* or hard-shell gourd. These come in an amazing variety of shapes and sizes from the long, slender "dipper gourds" to the large, aptly named "basketball gourds."

Like their relatives the squash, cucumber, melon, and pumpkin, gourds grow on long, running vines and take up a fair amount of space. They thrive in rich mounds of soil spaced 5 to 10 feet apart. When the fruit are developing, they demand a great deal of water.

Gourd Wise Men, see page 130

Because they are virtually waterlogged by the time they mature, they must be dried, or seasoned, before they can be used. During seasoning, they lose a phenomenal portion of their weight—huge, 100-pound gourds weigh only a few pounds when cured—and the green skin hardens to a woody, waterproof shell that can be carved, sanded, burned, painted, and finished much like wood.

To season gourds, place them on a rack or on several boards spaced several inches apart. Indoors or outdoors will do, as long as air can circulate freely. Aside from turning them occasionally, you can simply leave them alone for three to six months. When dry, gourds turn beige, brown, or off-white, and their seeds rattle when the gourd is shaken.

❦ Crafting with Pine Needles ❦

Pine needle crafting dates back to pre-Columbian times, when Native Americans coiled the needles into baskets and treated the containers with pine resin to make them waterproof.

Several varieties of pines produce needles 8 to 12 inches long—long enough to use effectively in

Pine Needle Broom Ornament, see page 197

craft projects. The needles of the longleaf pine *(Pinus palustris)*, one of the most common pines, are among the most widely available. Other common varieties include the slash pine *(Pinus Elliottii)*, loblolly pine *(Pinus taeda)*, and ponderosa pine *(Pinus ponderosa)*.

Midsummer to late fall is the best time to collect pine needles after they have matured, turned brown, and fallen from the tree. Look for recently fallen needles, which will be more pliable and a lighter brown than their older, stiffer colleagues. Select only whole pine needle clusters that are straight and completely dry; discard ones with broken or overly dry ends.

Soften and sterilize the needles by placing them in a large pot or heat-proof bowl and pouring enough boiling water over them to cover. Allow them to sit for 30 minutes to 1 hour, depending on their stiffness and the degree of flexibility your project requires. For example, they'll need to be extremely pliable if you plan to braid them, less flexible if you plan merely to bend them into a U shape for a miniature broom. Wrap the needles in a damp towel for 2 to 3 hours maximum; longer than that and they'll mildew.

Check the instructions for the project you plan to make to see whether the caps should be removed or left on. The caps can be pulled off with your fingers or popped off with a dull-edged knife.

❊ MAKING BOWS ❊

A simple two-loop bow—the kind we were all so proud of the day we learned to tie our shoes—can be exactly the right touch for a Christmas craft, especially if the ribbon is handsome and the project is small. The sachets on page 134 are decorated with simple two-loop bows, for example.

Taking that old technique one small step further, you can make an elongated, tailored bow by adding an extra loop to each side of a two-loop bow, then forming a circle of ribbon for the center (see Figure 22). Insert a precut 10-inch piece of fine-gauge floral wire through the center loop and twist the ends together on the back side of the bow. The maple pod wreath on page 128 displays such a bow to advantage.

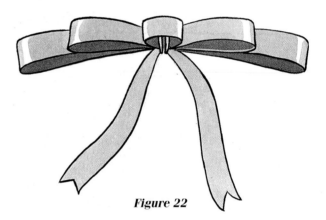

Figure 22

Another option, almost equally simple, is to make a bow by wiring individual loops of ribbon to floral picks. To begin, shape a length of ribbon into the size loop you want and cut off a piece of ribbon about 1 inch longer than that. Form a loop with the piece of ribbon and position its ends on either side of the pick. Wrap the pick's wire around both ribbon ends and the pick itself. Using this method, you can make single loops, double loops, and loops with tails (see Figure 23).

To make the kind of full bow that dresses up many a craft project, cut a piece of ribbon 10 inches long and trim each end on the diagonal. This length of ribbon will become one of the bow's streamers. Crimp the ribbon in the middle and hold it tightly between your thumb and index finger (see Figure 24).

Now begin making loops, working with a partially unrolled spool of ribbon. Create a second streamer that crosses over the first length of ribbon and crimp it in the middle. Form a 4- to 5-inch loop above the crimped point and a second similar loop

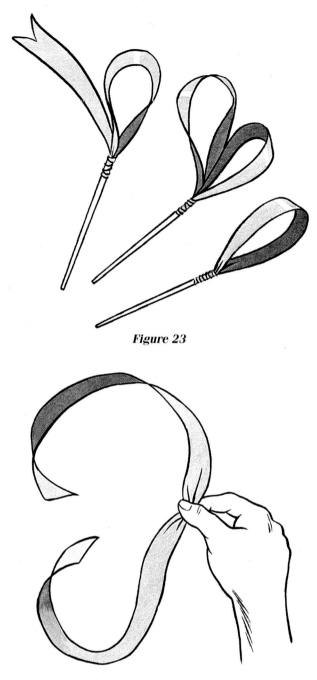

Figure 23

Figure 24

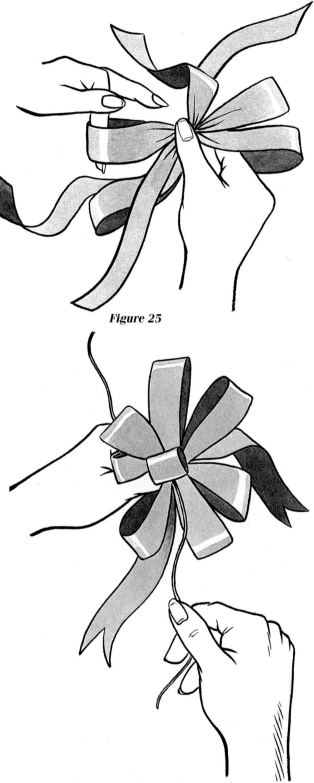

a precut, 12-inch length of thin-gauge floral wire through the finger loop and tightly twist both ends of the wire together on the back side of the bow.

To shape the bow, insert your finger through one loop at a time and pull it into position. If you grasp the loop by pinching it closed, it will flatten.

Figure 25

Figure 26

below the crimped point (see Figure 25).

Add additional top and bottom loops similar to the first ones, building them side by side instead of on top of each other and maintaining a firm grip on the center of the bow.

When the bottom layer of the bow looks as full as you'd like it to be, start adding a second layer in the same fashion, making the loops about 1 inch shorter than those in the bottom layer. To finish the bow, form a small finger loop by wrapping the ribbon over the finger you're using to hold your bow together (see Figure 26). Cut the ribbon the same length and at the same angle as the first streamer (assuming you want symmetrical streamers). Insert

THE PROJECTS

❧ Welcome, Christmas! ❧

Perhaps more than any other
holiday, the Christmas season
brings guests to our door.
Friends and family arrive with
gifts, hugs, and high hopes for
the good spirits, good company,
and good times to be found
inside. Welcome them before
they cross the threshold!
A wreath on the door, a swag
on the lamppost, or a garland
on the banister sets a festive
mood from the start.

Lotus Pod and Pomegranate Wreath

Pomegranates add a nice touch of color to this front door wreath, and small golden angels set a seasonal theme. The exotic-looking lotus pods will guarantee that your guests will have something to talk about as they make their entrance.

Materials

20-inch evergreen wreath

4 lotus pods, 5 inches in diameter

12 pomegranates

12 cedar "roses" (available at craft supply stores)

24 sprigs of baby's-breath, 3 to 5 inches long

Hot-glue gun and glue sticks

2 golden angels, 6 inches tall

Medium-gauge floral wire

8 feet of gold beaded cord

Wire cutters or heavy-duty scissors

Gold glitter spray

Floral fixative spray

1. Visualizing the evergreen wreath base as the face of a clock, hot-glue the lotus pods at 3, 6, 9, and 12 o'clock.

2. Hot-glue the angels to the wreath at 5 and 10 o'clock, nestling the angels down into the greenery.

3. Wire one end of the beaded cord to the back of the wreath at 12 o'clock. Working clockwise, wrap the cord around the wreath in a spiral fashion. When you return to your starting point, wire that end of the cord to the back of the wreath and clip off any extra cord.

4. Hot-glue the pomegranates randomly around the wreath, occasionally clustering two or three of them.

5. Spray touches of gold glitter onto the cedar roses and allow them to dry briefly. Hot-glue the roses to the wreath, distributing them evenly.

6. Hot-glue the baby's-breath randomly around the wreath.

7. Spray the wreath with floral fixative.

Wheat Swag

Wheat bundles are age-old symbols of abundance—an inviting greeting for the hungry dinner guests at your front door. If you hang the swag in the yard, hungry birds will find it equally inviting and will promptly eat all the wheat seeds.

Materials

35 stalks of wheat, twenty-five 30 inches long and ten 24 inches long

3 sprigs of pepperberries, 6 inches long

Dried lichen, 3 inches in diameter

1 dried mushroom

24 inches of heavy-gauge floral wire, cut into two 5-inch pieces and two 7-inch pieces

Wire cutters

2 yards of metallic patterned ribbon, 2 inches wide

Hot-glue gun and glue sticks

1. Arrange the 30-inch wheat stalks in a bouquet and secure them around the middle with a 5-inch piece of floral wire.

2. Arrange the 24-inch wheat stalks in a bouquet and secure them in the same way.

3. Place the shorter bouquet on top of the larger one and wire them together with a 7-inch piece of wire, forming a loop for hanging as you twist.

4. Make a bow with the patterned ribbon and wire it to the wheat with the remaining 7-inch piece of wire, positioning it to cover the wires. (See "Making Bows" on page 30.)

5. Hot-glue the pepperberry sprigs and the lichen among the ribbon loops; then hot-glue the mushroom under the ribbon.

This simple-to-make cedar swag (see page 44) and twig wreath (see page 42) can be displayed outdoors.

Twig Wreath

*Constructed of water-resistant materials, this
cheerful wreath can grace a lamppost or shutter.*

Materials

20 cedar stems, 4 to 5 inches long

10 Fraser fir stems, 5 inches long

45 pieces of white annual statice, 2 inches
    in diameter

Medium-gauge floral wire

Wire cutters

14-inch-diameter twig wreath base

Hot-glue gun and glue sticks

3 yards of waterproof red velvet ribbon,
    ½ inch wide, cut into three
      1-yard pieces

1. With the medium-gauge wire, make a hanger for the wreath. (See "Making Hangers" on page 22.)

2. Hot-glue the cedar stems into the wreath base, positioning them to slant in the same direction as the twigs in the base.

3. Hot-glue the Fraser fir stems into the wreath, again following the direction of the twigs and spacing the fir tips evenly around the wreath.

4. Hot-glue the statice around the inside of the wreath.

5. Make three bows from the red velvet ribbon and wire them equidistantly around the wreath. (See "Making Bows" on page 30.)

Cedar Swag

Simple arrangements are often the most satisfying. This handsome swag takes about an hour to make and will dress up your front porch or door.

Materials

2 pinecones, about 2 inches long

6 stems of cedar, 12 inches long

8-inch frond of plumosa fern

White acrylic paint

½-inch flat paintbrush

4 yards of waterproof red velvet ribbon, 2½ inches wide

Medium-gauge floral wire

Wire cutters or heavy-duty scissors

Hot-glue gun and glue sticks

1. Bake the cones at 200°F for 25 minutes to kill any insect eggs or larvae.

2. Paint the tips of the pinecone petals with white acrylic paint and set them aside to dry.

3. With the red velvet ribbon, make a nine-loop bow with 18-inch streamers. (See "Making Bows" on page 30.)

4. Wire the pinecones into the center of the bow. (See "Floral Wire" on page 17 for wiring instructions.)

5. Place the cedar stems end to end, over-lapping them by 2 inches, and wire the stems together.

6. Using the wire cutters or heavy-duty scissors, cut a 30-inch piece of medium-gauge wire and wire the bow over the center of the swag, leaving two long wire tails for attaching the arrangement to its ultimate location.

7. Hot-glue the fern to the bow, tucking the ends under the pinecones.

Braided Raffia Swag

This vertical swag looks handsome indoors or out. Keep it looking its best outdoors by hanging it where it has some protection from the elements.

Materials

7 pinecones, 6 to 8 inches long (the cones in the photo are from a white pine)

9 pinecones, 3 to 4 inches long

10 stems of Fraser fir, 6 to 9 inches long

8 sprigs of German statice, 3 to 5 inches long

2 yards of red twisted-paper ribbon

Medium-gauge floral wire

Wire cutters or heavy-duty scissors

Purchased braided-raffia swag, 30 inches long

14 strands of red raffia, 2 yards long

2 artificial hanging bird's nests, 3 to 4 inches in diameter

Small handful of excelsior

Hot-glue gun and glue sticks

2 artificial red birds, 2 to 3 inches from beak to tail

Floral picks

1. Bake the pinecones at 200°F for 25 minutes to kill any insect eggs or larvae.

2. Loop the twisted-paper ribbon into a double figure 8 and wire it to the top of the swag using the medium-gauge wire.

3. Make a bow with ten strands of red raffia and wire it over the center of the twisted-paper figure 8s. (See "Making Bows" on page 30.)

4. Thread an 8-inch piece of wire into and then back out of the back of one of the bird's nests and wire it to the swag. Repeat this process with the other nest.

5. Place a small clump of excelsior into each nest and hot-glue an artificial bird on top.

6. Make a bow with the remaining four strands of red raffia and wire it to the swag underneath the lower bird's nest.

7. Wire the white pinecones evenly over the swag. If necessary, use hot glue to hold the cones where you want them.

8. Wire together three of the nine assorted cones. Repeat twice more so that you have three groups of three wired cones. Wire the groups to the swag, holding them in place with hot glue as necessary.

9. Attach each stem of Fraser fir to a floral pick. (See "Floral Picks" on page 16.) Put a dab of hot glue on the end of the pick and pick the fir stem into the swag. Repeat the process with the remaining stems, positioning them so that the fir branches seem to "fall" down the swag.

10. Hot-glue sprigs of German statice randomly down the swag.

This braided raffia swag (see page 45) and braided pine needle wreath (see page 48) welcome holiday guests to your home.

Braided Pine Needle Wreath

Protected from the weather by a healthy coat of shellac, this stunning wreath makes a perfect outdoor decoration.

Materials

355 longleaf pine needle clusters, caps on, divided into one group of 310 and one group of 45

Large pot or heat-proof bowl

Boiling water

Towel

Brown quilting thread

Scissors

8½-inch-diameter wire wreath base with 5-inch opening in the center

Needle

1-inch flat paintbrush

Shellac

28 inches of red ribbon, ¹⁄₁₆ inch wide

1. Put the pine needles into the pot and pour boiling water over them to cover. Allow the needles to soak for approximately 1 hour. Pour off the water and wrap the needles in a towel to keep them soft and pliable.

2. Tie six pine needle clusters together with the quilting thread just under their caps, making a strong double knot.

3. Divide the bundle evenly into three groups.

4. Braid the needles four times—that is, bring the right group of needles over the center group, then the left group over the center group, then the right over the center, then the left over the center.

5. Insert two extra pine needles into the braid, positioning them over the right group and under the center one, with their caps pointing to the right and protruding from the braid about ¼ inch (see Figure 1). The main body of the added needles should always be to the left of the braid.

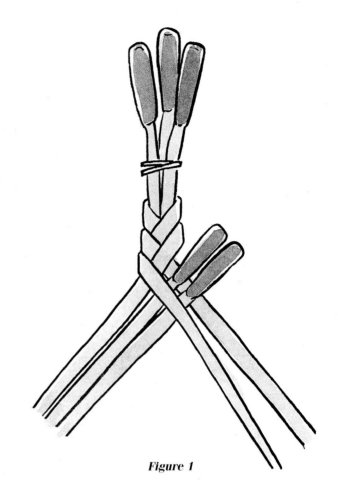

Figure 1

6. Continue braiding, inserting two extra pine needles into the braid in a similar fashion after every four braids until you have used the 310 needle clusters and have a continuous braid about 9 feet long. As you near the end of the braid, continue to braid without adding extra needles; the last 4 or 5 inches of the braid will taper off and will blend smoothly into the wreath. Tie off the end of the braid with the thread.

7. Tie a piece of thread about 1 yard long to the inner rim of the wreath base and thread the other end through the needle.

8. Starting with the end of the braid you first worked on, lay the braid against the inner rim of the wreath base. Leaving the first 2 inches of the braid hanging free, bring the needle through the braid from back to front, close to the edge of the braid. Bring the thread around the edge of the braid, around the wire frame, and back through the braid, again sewing from back to front (see Figure 2 on page 50). Try to conceal the thread in the braid. Continue to make whipstitches about ¼ inch apart until the inner rim of the base is covered.

9. When you are 3 or 4 inches from the end of your thread, tie another 1-yard piece of thread to it in a double knot, close enough to the work so that the knot can be pulled to the outside of the coil. The next coil will hide the knot.

10. Sew the second coil of the braid to the first, whipstitching the two coils together as closely as possible to their edges.

11. Continue stitching coils to previous ones, taking the thread around the wire base whenever possible. Tuck the very end of the braid behind the back of the wreath.

12. Tuck the 2-inch tail on the inner rim to the back of the wreath and secure it in place with a couple of stitches. Or, as shown in the photo, bring it up and over the top of the wreath and stitch it in place.

13. Use the paintbrush to coat the wreath with shellac, both front and back.

14. To make a bow for the wreath, make a 28-inch braid with the group of 45 needle clusters, following the instructions in Steps 1 through 6 with two exceptions: First, tie the $\frac{1}{16}$-inch ribbon to the six pine needles used to begin the braid and braid it in with the needles. Second, add only one extra pine needle after every four braids.

15. Shape the 28-inch braid into a two-loop bow with two streamers the same length. Rather than knotting the bow, stitch through the layers of braid with the quilting thread to hold them together.

16. Paint the bow with shellac and allow it to dry.

17. Attach the bow to the wreath with needle and thread.

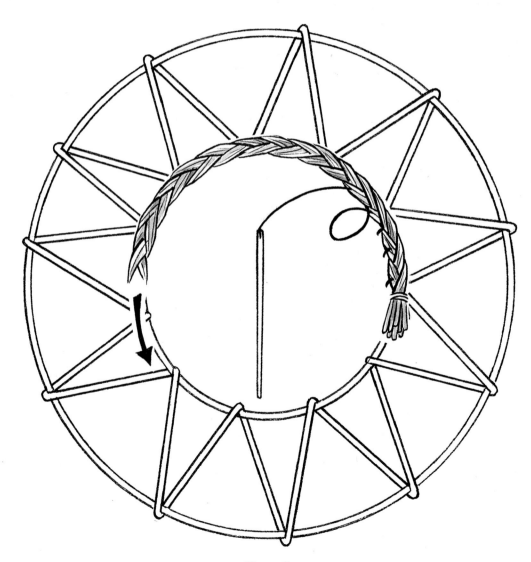

Figure 2

Hanging Holiday Basket

*Since this arrangement is equally attractive
from front and back, it's a perfect decoration
to hang from the front porch light.*

Materials

1 pinecone, 6 to 7 inches long

9 pinecones, 1 to 2 inches long

2 artificial apples

6 sprigs of Fraser fir, two 6 inches long and four 4 inches long

8 to 10 pieces of boxwood, 6 inches long

4 pieces of ming fern, 3 inches long

3 clusters of artificial red berries, 2 inches in diameter

4 sprays of dried white larkspur, 4 inches long

Pruning shears

Grapevine basket without handle, 8 inches in diameter and 4 inches tall

3⅔ yards of red velvet ribbon, ¾ inch wide, cut into one 40-inch piece and one 2½-yard piece

15 strands of raffia, 1 yard long

Medium-gauge floral wire

Wire cutters or heavy-duty scissors

1½ yards of red velvet ribbon, 3⁄16 inch wide

Hot-glue gun and glue sticks

1. Bake the pinecones at 200°F for 25 minutes to kill any insect eggs or larvae.

2. Using the pruning shears, cut away the bottom of the basket.

3. Turn the basket on its side and thread the 40-inch piece of the wide ribbon through the new "top" of the basket to make a hanger. Tie the ends in a knot and position the knot at the top of the basket.

4. Make three raffia bows (see "Making Bows" on page 30), using five stands for each bow. On one bow, make 2-foot-long streamers.

5. Wire the bow with the long streamers to the new "bottom" of the basket. Wire a second bow to the top of the basket near the hanger, and the third to the "floor" inside the basket.

6. Make a bow with the 1½ yards of narrow red ribbon and wire it to the top of the basket on top of the raffia bow, covering the hanger's knot.

7. Make a bow with the 2½-yard piece of wide ribbon and wire it inside the basket on top of the raffia bow.

8. Hot-glue one apple to the top of the basket, positioning it toward the back of the arrangement. Hot-glue the other apple inside the basket among the loops of the bow.

9. Hot-glue the four shorter sprigs of Fraser fir around the bows on top of the basket. Hot-glue the remaining fir around the bows inside the basket.

10. Hot-glue the boxwood pieces around the bows on top of the basket and around the bows on the inside.

11. Hot-glue the pieces of ming fern to the arrangement, dividing them between the top and the inside.

12. Hot-glue one berry cluster to the top of the basket, positioning it toward the front. Hot-glue a second cluster to the bottom of the basket, as shown in the photo, and a third cluster on the bottom of the back of the basket, diagonally across from the lower berries shown in the photo.

13. Hot-glue two sprays of larkspur to the top of the basket and two sprays inside.

14. Place the large cone inside the raffia bow on the underside of the basket and tie the raffia streamers in a knot under the cone.

15. Hot-glue three small cones to the top of the basket to help conceal the hanger knot. Hot-glue six small cones to the raffia streamers, as shown in the photo.

Santa Greeting Gourds

With a handsome Santa or two by your front door,
guests will feel instantly welcome, suddenly festive,
and decidedly fortunate to have been invited.

Materials

2 seasoned bottle gourds,
about 12 inches tall
(See "Using Gourds"
on page 29.)

Soap

Water

Steel wool

Pencil

Acrylic paints in assorted colors

1-inch flat paintbrush

1½-inch flat paintbrush

Clear varnish

1. Soak the gourds in soapy water for 20 minutes and use the steel wool to scrub off all dirt and mold. Allow to dry completely.

2. Sketch your design on the gourds in pencil, using Figure 1 (see page 56) and Figure 2 (see page 57) as guides.

3. Paint the gourds in whatever colors you desire, using the 1-inch paintbrush. Use one color at a time and allow each color to dry before proceeding with the next.

4. After all paint is completely dry, use the 1½-inch paintbrush to apply a heavy coat of clear varnish to the gourds to help keep out the moisture.

Figure 1

Figure 2

Spiral Garland

Although this 5-foot-long garland is a rather ambitious project, the grapevine base can be used for years to come. Hang it on your front porch where it will twist gracefully in the winter wind.

Materials

36 feet of grapevine in varying lengths

9 stems of white pine, 10 to 14 inches long

8 stems of cedar, 10 to 14 inches long

8 stems of boxwood, 10 to 14 inches long

5 small red apples

10 sprigs of red canella berries

10 garlic bulbs

20 button mushrooms, 1 inch in diameter

5 mushrooms, 4 to 5 inches in diameter

1 wasp nest (optional)

12 feet of heavy-gauge wire (not floral wire)

Floral spool wire

Wire cutters

Hot-glue gun and glue sticks

4 yards of white satin ribbon, ¼ inch wide

4 yards of gold mesh ribbon, 2 inches wide

Craft picks

Note: Vine-covered spiral bases can be purchased in many craft stores. If none is available in your area, you can make your own by following Steps 1 through 5.

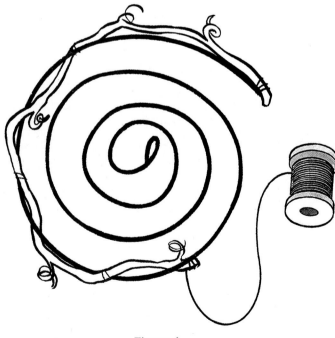

Figure 1

1. Soak the grapevines in warm water overnight to soften them.

2. Take the heavy-gauge wire and twist 2 inches of one end of the wire into a loop to serve as a hanger.

3. Coil the wire with the hanging loop to the inside. The outer circle of the coil should be about 2 feet in diameter.

4. Select three lengths of grapevine and hold them as a bundle with their ends even at one end. Attach the grapevine to the heavy-gauge wire coil by wrapping with the spool wire (see Figure 1). When a piece of grapevine ends, add a new piece of vine, pushing it 3 or 4 inches into the previous vines.

5. Coil the grapevine-covered base as tightly as you can to make the coil flat. Place a stack of books on the coil for several days to hold it in this shape.

6. Hang the grapevine base where you can work on all sides of it. Starting at the top, hot-glue stems of pine, cedar, and boxwood into the base, alternating the evergreen varieties and covering the base well.

7. Hot-glue the ribbons to the top of the base and arrange them down the length of the garland, weaving them in and out of the greenery.

8. Insert a craft pick into each of the five apples and hot-glue the picks into the grapevine base. Distribute the apples evenly down the garland.

9. Hot-glue the remaining materials to the garland, spacing them attractively and leaving no large areas bare.

Artemisia Crescent

*On this distinctive decoration for the door,
sober green ferns and subdued gray artemisia
contrast nicely with a gilded pinecone and
flashy red floral buttons.*

Materials

1 longleaf pinecone with 5-inch-diameter
    base, all petals intact and tightly closed

4 ounces of Spanish moss

60 stems of artemisia, 20 inches long

3 fronds of Australian fern

20 long-stemmed red floral buttons

Coping saw

Gold spray paint

Scrrated knife

36 × 12 × 2-inch block of floral foam

Wire cutters

Medium-gauge floral wire

Hot-glue gun and glue sticks

Floral pins

Craft pick

Heavy-duty scissors

1. Bake the cone at 200°F for 25 minutes to kill any insect eggs or larvae.

2. With the coping saw, cut off approximately the top seven-eighths of the cone and put it aside for a future craft project.

3. Spray paint the remaining bottom of the cone with the gold spray paint.

4. Using the serrated knife, cut the floral foam in a crescent 34 inches long and 10 inches high (see Figure 1).

5. Using the wire cutters, cut a 6-inch piece of medium-gauge floral wire to make a hanger for the arch. Bring the ends together and twist the wire several times near the center to create a loop about ¾ inch high. Trim the wire ends to about 1 inch and twist them together all the way to the end of the wires.

6. Position the hanger on the back of the foam, so that the loop projects over the arch and the hanger is exactly in the center of the curve. With the end of the hanger, pierce the foam at that point at a downward angle. Dab some hot glue on the end of the hanger and insert it into the hole. For extra stability, push two floral pins over the hanger and into the foam.

7. Cover the front and edges of the arch with the Spanish moss, attaching it with floral pins.

8. Cut the artemisia into pieces ranging from 8 to 20 inches long and insert them into the foam, with the stem ends at the center. Begin with the longest pieces and end with the shortest pieces. If necessary, attach any small fill-in pieces with floral pins or hot glue.

9. Cut an 18-inch length of wire. Wrap the wire around the pinecone, placing it underneath the row of petals closest to the cut side of the cone. When the wire has wrapped all the way around the cone, work both ends toward the center of the cone and twist them together tightly against the cone. Cut the wire tail to 2 inches. Place a craft pick against the wire tail, overlapping the two by about 1 inch, and hot-glue them together. Pick the pinecone, cut side down, into the center of the foam.

10. Using the scissors, cut the Australian ferns into individual leaves. Hot-glue the larger leaves horizontally, on both sides of the pinecone. Hot-glue the smaller leaves above and below the cone, making a spray of greenery around the cone.

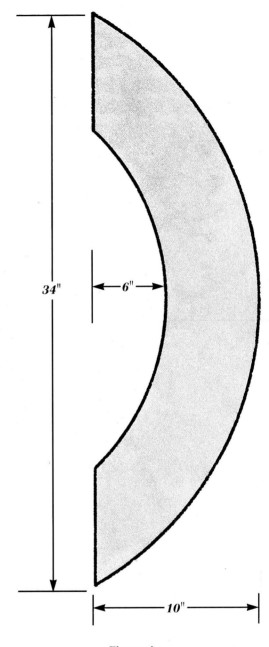

Figure 1

11. Carefully break the flower heads off the floral buttons, leaving a stem of about 2 inches on each flower, and set the flowers aside. Hot-glue the stems in a sunburst pattern around the cone, with the longer stems radiating out the sides and the shorter stems on the top and bottom.

12. Randomly hot-glue the floral button flowers stem side down to the ferns and the artemisia.

Birdseed Ornaments

Birds are among the best dinner guests. They don't spill gravy on your favorite tablecloth, and they never complain about the food. This simple recipe makes several festive birdseed ornaments, such as a Christmas stocking or wreath, that will keep feathered friends happy when they come to dine in your yard.

Materials

For six ornaments:

6 slices of bread
Stocking-shaped cookie cutter, or cutters in
    assorted Christmas shapes
Pastry brush
3 egg whites
2 cups of mixed birdseed
Aluminum foil
Cookie sheet
Wire cutters or heavy-duty scissors
Fine-gauge floral wire
6 assorted ribbons, 10 to 14 inches long
Hot-glue gun and glue sticks

1. Place a slice of bread on a scar-proof work surface. Using the cookie cutter, cut out a stocking-shaped piece of bread. Save the stocking and set aside the rest of the slice of bread for later use, such as for making bread crumbs. Repeat this process five more times. To make a wreath-shaped ornament, use a doughnut cutter or two biscuit cutters, one larger than the other, to cut out the bread.

2. With the pastry brush, brush a layer of egg white onto the bread cutouts.

3. Press a thick layer of birdseed onto each cutout.

4. Bake the ornaments at 350°F for 10 minutes on an aluminum-foil–covered baking sheet. Allow them to cool completely.

5. To make hangers for the ornaments, use the wire cutters or scissors to cut six 7-inch pieces of floral wire. Gently insert the end of a wire through the top of each ornament, at least ¼ inch from the edge. Form a loop with each wire and twist the wire ends together to secure.

6. Tie the ribbons into simple bows and hot-glue them in place over the twisted wires.

*Spectacular Fraser firs provide a breathtaking
backdrop for birdseed ornaments (see page 64).*

Pinecone Swag

*Our hearts may belong to red and green at Christmastime,
but we can still fancy a fling with a different color. This simple
swag offers a taste of peach along with traditional pinecones.*

Materials

3 pinecones, one 5 inches long,
    one 4½ inches long, and
    one 3½ inches long

12 pieces of preserved ruscus,
    2 inches long

20 pieces of German statice, 1 inch long

4 to 6 clusters of tiny, dried, peach-colored
    flowers, ½ inch in diameter

Polyurethane spray

Hot-glue gun and glue sticks

3¾ yards of peach grosgrain ribbon, 1 inch
    wide, cut into one 2-yard piece, one
    25-inch piece, one 18-inch piece,
    and one 13-inch piece

Floral pick

Floral pins

Medium-gauge floral wire

Wire cutters

2 × 2-inch piece of wood, ¼ to ½ inch
    thick

Scissors

1. Bake the cones at 200°F for 25 minutes to kill any insect eggs or larvae. Allow the cones to cool and then spray them with the polyurethane.

2. Hot-glue the ruscus, German statice, and peach flowers randomly around the cones. Since the cones will hang with their bases uppermost, hold them that way while working.

3. Fold under ¼ inch of one end of the 25-inch piece of ribbon and hot-glue the folded strip to the center of the largest cone, positioning the folded tab so that it is not visible from the front of the arrangement. Use the floral pick to hold the ribbon against the cone until the glue has set.

4. Trim the "legs" of the floral pins to ½ inch. Insert one of the pins through the glued ribbon and into the cone for extra security.

5. Repeat Steps 3 and 4 twice more, attaching the 18-inch ribbon to the middle-sized cone and the 13-inch ribbon to the smallest cone.

6. To make a hanger, cut a 22-inch length of medium gauge floral wire with the wire cutters and form a loop with tails about 8 inches long. Twist the wires together right under the loop. Wrap the wire ends around the block of wood. To secure the hanger, twist all wires together just under the loop.

7. Hot-glue the end of the longest ribbon to the center of the piece of wood. Hot-glue the medium ribbon to the right and the shortest ribbon to the left.

8. Using the 2-yard piece of ribbon, make a bow with 6-inch streamers (see "Making Bows" on page 30), wiring the bow around its center. Cut the streamer ends on the diagonal.

9. Hot-glue the bow to the wood, covering the ends of the hanging ribbons.

*Simple, graceful pinecone swags (see page 68)
add festive touches to your holiday home.*

White Pine Decorations

A white pine wreath and swag (see page 76) spread Christmas cheer to your home's facade. All materials are impervious to rain and snow, making perfect outdoor decorations.

Door Wreath

Materials

6 pinecones, 8 inches long

30-inch-diameter grapevine wreath base

6 stems of white pine, 10 inches long

4 stems of canella berries, 6 to 8 inches long

1 piece of dried lichen, 4 inches in diameter

12 stems of caspia, 10 inches long

3 yards of wired gold net ribbon, 3 inches wide

Medium-gauge floral wire

Wire cutters or heavy-duty scissors

Hot-glue gun and glue sticks

1. Bake the pinecones at 200°F for 25 minutes to kill any insect eggs or larvae.

2. Tie the gold ribbon in a bow with 18-inch streamers (see "Making Bows" on page 30) and wire it to one side of the wreath base. Shape the streamers into gentle curves around the sides of the base.

3. Hot-glue five of the stems of pine to the wreath base to the left of the bow and glue the remaining pine stems under the ribbon streamers to the right of the bow.

4. Wire the pinecones together in pairs. Trim off excess wire ends and hot-glue the cones to the wreath.

5. Hot-glue the canella berries to the left of the bow and opposite the bow and hot-glue the lichen opposite the bow.

6. Hot-glue the caspia stems evenly around the wreath.

(continued on page 76)

*These white pine decorations (see page 72)
invite holiday visitors into your home.*

Lamp Swag

Materials

3 pinecones, 7 to 8 inches long

9 stems of white pine, three 4 feet long, three 3½ feet long, and three 3 feet long

1 stem of canella berries, 8 inches long

2 stems of caspia, 10 inches long

Medium-gauge floral wire

Wire cutters

2½ yards of wired gold net ribbon, 3 inches wide

Hot-glue gun and glue sticks

1. Bake the pinecones at 200°F for 25 minutes to kill any insect eggs or larvae.

2. Gather the 4-foot stems of pine into a bouquet and wrap the stems about 8 inches from the cut ends with the floral wire. In the same manner, make two more bouquets: one with the 3½-foot stems of pine, and one with the 3-foot stems of pine.

3. Gather the three pine bouquets together, with the cut ends even, and with the longest bouquet on the bottom and the shortest bouquet on top. Wire the three bouquets together about 8 inches from their cut ends, bending the wire ends into a loop to serve as a hanger.

4. Tie the ribbon in a bow (see "Making Bows" on page 30) and wire it to the swag with the medium-gauge wire, positioning it to cover the bouquet wires. Wire the pinecones around the bow.

5. Hot-glue the berries and the caspia in place, tucking about 1 inch of their stems under the bow.

Pinecone Wreath

Part of the charm of this cone wreath is its symmetrical precision: The right and left halves are virtually identical. Place it on a front door, a gate, or a lamppost as a cheerful welcome.

Materials

2 longleaf pinecones, one with a 4-inch-
diameter base and one with a 2-inch-
diameter base

76 sweet gum seedpods

10 Norway spruce cones, 5½ inches long

28 Virginia pinecones

20 black spruce cones, 1 inch long and 1 inch
in diameter

2 large stems of German statice, cut into small
pieces

Medium-gauge floral wire

Wire cutters

Coping saw

Pruning shears

Wire wreath base, 18 inches in diameter

Electric drill with ¹⁄₁₆-inch bit

Needle-nosed pliers

Hot-glue gun and glue sticks

Polyurethane spray

Serrated knife

5 × 5 × ¾-inch block of floral foam

4 yards of red velvet ribbon, 2 inches wide,
cut into two 17-inch pieces, five 12-
inch pieces, and five 10-inch pieces

Floral picks

Scissors

1. Bake the cones and sweet gum seedpods at 200°F for 25 minutes to kill any insect eggs or larvae.

2. Form a hanger for the wreath from a piece of the medium-gauge wire. (See "Making Hangers" on page 22.)

3. Using the coping saw, remove the top one-half to three-fourths of each longleaf pinecone by sawing between two rows of petals. Discard the cutoff tops of the cones.

4. With the pruning shears, trim the uppermost row of petals on one longleaf cone as close to the cone's core as possible. On the second row, cut off the outer three-fourths of the petals. On the third row, cut off the outer half of the petals. On the fourth row, cut off the outer one-fourth. Repeat the process with the other longleaf cone.

5. Wire the larger longleaf cone flower to the bottom center of the wreath base. Wire the smaller flower to the top center of the wreath base. (See "Floral Wire" on page 17.)

6. Wire six Norway spruce cones around the inside of the base, three on each side.

7. Wire the remaining four Norway spruce cones to the bottom of the wreath. Position two of them on the outside of the base on either side of the cone flower. Position the other two immediately above the first two.

8. Wire the Virginia pinecones around the base, to the outside of the Norway spruce cones. Leave openings at the top and bottom of the base.

9. Using the electric drill and ¹⁄₁₆-inch bit, drill through the center of each sweet gum seedpod. Insert a 6-inch piece of wire through each hole and wire the seedpods around the outside of the wreath, leaving an opening at the bottom. Use the photo as a guide.

10. Check to make sure that all the cones are firmly attached; rewire or reattach any loose ones. Using the needle-nosed pliers, bend any wire ends to the back of the base.

11. Hot-glue the black spruce cones to the wreath, using the photo as a guide. Place four between the Norway spruce cones at the bottom left of the wreath and four more between the cones at the bottom right. Place three above the cone flower at the top of the wreath. Place one at each juncture of the Norway spruce cones on the inside of the wreath. Place the last four at the tips of the top Norway spruce cones at the bottom of the wreath.

12. Spray all the cones and pods with polyurethane and allow them to dry.

13. At the bottom of the wreath there will be a pocket of empty space behind the pinecone flower, where the wreath base and the attached cones fail to fit tightly. Measure that pocket, use the serrated knife to cut the floral foam to fit it, and insert the foam into the space. Secure it with hot glue if necessary.

14. To make streamers for the bow, attach each 17-inch piece of ribbon to a floral pick. (See "Making Bows" on page 30.) Pick the streamers into the foam block at the bottom of the wreath. Trim the ends on the diagonal.

15. Form the remaining pieces of ribbon into loops and pick them into the foam to form a bow.

16. Hot-glue pieces of statice around the wreath, using the photo as a guide.

❧ Deck the Halls ❧

With boughs of holly,
with branches of evergreens,
with clusters of berries,
with ribbons and flowers and
fruit, with pinecones, seedpods,
and every other beautiful
Christmas gift that nature has
bestowed. Living room and guest
room, playroom and powder
room—your whole house can
be graced by the spirit of
Christmas.

Topiaries

Until recently, topiaries languished in Victorian obscurity, long forgotten or dismissed as fussy relics of an ornate era. With the revival of interest in dried flower crafts, they have sprung back into life, graced with brighter colors and simpler lines.

Rose Topiary

Materials

¼-inch-diameter twig, 9 inches long

1 square foot of garden moss

3 pieces of grapevine, ⅛ inch in diameter and 8 inches long

120 dried red roses, ¼ inch long, with leaves

3-inch-diameter clay flowerpot, 2½ inches high

Aluminum foil

Plaster of paris

Water

2½-inch-diameter foam ball

Hot-glue gun and glue sticks

1 yard of green velvet ribbon, ¼ inch wide

1. Line the flowerpot with the aluminum foil.

2. Mix the plaster of paris with water, following the package instructions to make 1 cup. Pour the plaster into the flowerpot and insert the twig into the plaster, holding the twig upright until the plaster is dry enough to hold it securely. Allow the plaster to set completely.

3. Cover the foam ball with moss, attaching it with dabs of hot glue.

4. Push the moss-covered foam ball down over the twig so the twig is inserted snugly.

5. Hot-glue one end of each piece of vine to the plaster at the base of the twig. Twist the vines around the twig once and insert their other ends into the foam ball.

6. Hot-glue the roses to the ball, covering it as completely as possible.

7. Hot-glue small pieces of moss between the roses to fill any gaps.

8. Hot-glue moss over the plaster in the flowerpot, covering it completely.

9. Make a bow with 6-inch streamers from the green velvet ribbon and hot-glue it to the base of the ball. (See "Making Bows" on page 30.)

Tiny Topiary

Materials

¼-inch-diameter twig, 7 inches long

8 square inches of garden moss

18 cockscomb heads, 1 inch in diameter

12 white strawflowers

18 sprigs of pepperberries, 1 inch in diameter

4 dried red roses

28 sprigs of boxwood, 1 inch long

2¼-inch-diameter clay flowerpot, 2¼ inches high

Aluminum foil

Plaster of paris

Water

2-inch-diameter foam ball

Hot-glue gun and glue sticks

½ yard of plaid ribbon, ¾ inch wide

1. Line the flowerpot with the aluminum foil.

2. Mix the plaster of paris with water, following the package instructions to make ½ cup. Pour the plaster into the flowerpot and insert the twig into the plaster, holding the twig upright until the plaster is dry enough to hold it securely. Allow the plaster to set completely.

3. Cover the foam ball with moss, attaching it with dabs of hot glue.

4. Push the moss-covered foam ball down over the twig so the twig is inserted snugly.

5. Hot-glue the floral materials to the moss-covered ball, distributing them evenly and covering the ball completely.

6. Hot-glue moss over the plaster in the flowerpot, covering it completely.

7. Make a bow with 3-inch streamers and hot-glue it to the base of the ball. (See "Making Bows" on page 30.)

Blooming Candle

With its vivid red berries, bright green boxwood, and frosted blue juniper, this fresh arrangement adds Christmas color to a sideboard, breakfast table, or mantelpiece.

Materials

- 100 sprigs of boxwood, 3 inches long
- 12 sprigs of 'Blue Rug' juniper, 6 inches long
- 2 pieces of ivy, 8 inches long
- 9 sprigs of dusty miller, 3 inches long
- 8 small sumac heads
- Large jar
- Floral picks
- Serrated knife
- 1 block of wet floral foam
- 1 white candle, 6 inches high and 3 inches in diameter
- Saucer or shallow bowl
- Floral tape
- Hot-glue gun and glue sticks

1. Place the stems of boxwood, juniper, ivy, and dusty miller in a jar of water overnight to hydrate.

2. Attach two or three sprigs of boxwood to a floral pick. Continue in this manner until you have 35 mini bouquets of boxwood.

3. With the serrated knife, cut off one end of the foam block to make a block that is 5 inches square. Set aside the small left-over piece for a future project.

4. In the middle of the square piece of foam, cut a well ½ inch deep and 3 inches wide. Insert the candle and check to see that it fits snugly. Remove the candle and trim the corners off the foam to round it out a bit. Soak it in water until it is saturated.

5. Drain the wet foam and place it in the saucer or shallow bowl. Tape the foam to the saucer with the floral tape.

6. Insert 11 of the juniper sprigs directly into the foam, first stripping off some of the bottom leaves if a longer stem is necessary. Insert the stems at the same angle as you work around the base. To create a circle, insert the stems deeper into the foam at the ends and the corners of the rectangle and more shallowly at the sides.

7. Pick in the boxwood evenly around the base, working at the same angle and maintaining a circular shape. Cover the entire surface of the foam except for the well.

8. Insert the dusty miller and six of the sumac heads into the foam, using the photo as a guide. Insert the two stems of ivy into the foam on opposite sides of the arrangement.

9. Place several dots of hot glue on the back of the remaining juniper sprig and attach it to the candle in a spiral pattern.

10. Divide the two remaining sumac heads into small clusters of three to six berries each. Hot-glue the clusters along the juniper sprig that is on the candle, placing the larger clusters at the bottom.

11. Set the candle in the well. Water the arrangement daily.

Gift-Wrapped Glycerin Soaps

Colorful glycerin soaps decorated with leaves and flowers make great presents for the hard-to-shop-for folks on your Christmas list.

Green Soap with Red Ribbon

Materials

5 alder cones or other tiny cones

5 sprigs of caspia, 1 to 1½ inches long

44 inches of red satin ribbon, ¼ inch wide, cut into one 16-inch piece and one 28-inch piece

Bar of green glycerin soap

Straight pins

Hot-glue gun and glue sticks

1. Using the 16-inch piece of ribbon, wrap the soap as you would a package—first end to end, then side to side. Insert straight pins through both layers of ribbon and into the soap where the ribbon overlaps to hold it in place.

2. Make a bow with the 28-inch piece of ribbon and pin it to the soap. (See "Making Bows" on page 30.)

3. Hot-glue the cones through the bow, using the photo as a guide.

4. Hot-glue the caspia around the bow.

Pink Soap with Lacy Ribbon

Materials

4 sprigs of ming fern, one 1 inch long and three 2 inches long

3 sprigs of pink-dyed baby's-breath, ½ inch in diameter

20 inches of pink-threaded lace ribbon, ½ inch wide, cut into two 10-inch pieces

Bar of pink glycerin soap

Straight pins

Hot-glue gun and glue sticks

1. With one piece of ribbon, wrap the soap as you would a package, first end to end, then side to side. Insert straight pins through both layers of ribbon and into the soap where the ribbon overlaps to hold it in place.

2. Make a two-loop bow with the other piece of ribbon and pin it to the soap.

3. Hot-glue the ming fern to the ribbon, using the photo as a guide.

4. Hot-glue the baby's-breath to the bow.

Purple Soap

Materials

Dried cream-and-pink rose with 1-inch stem

3 sprigs of boxwood, 1 to 2 inches long

3 sprigs of pepperberries, 1 to 1½ inches in diameter

42 inches of pink satin ribbon, ¼ inch wide, cut into two 11-inch pieces and two 10-inch pieces

Bar of purple glycerin soap

Straight pins

Hot-glue gun and glue sticks

1. Wrap one of the 11-inch pieces of ribbon around the edge of the soap, overlapping the ends. Insert a straight pin through both layers of ribbon and into the soap. Repeat the process with the other 11-inch piece of ribbon, using the photo as a guide.

2. Wrap one of the 10-inch pieces of ribbon around the soap from end to end and pin in place in a similar fashion. Repeat the process with the other 10-inch ribbon.

3. Insert the rose stem directly into the soap between the two top ribbons, positioning it in the center of the soap, as shown in the photo. If the stem is too weak to pierce the soap, hot-glue the rose to the ribbons.

4. Arrange the boxwood sprigs around the rose and hot-glue them to the ribbons.

5. Position the pepperberry sprigs around the rose and hot-glue them to the ribbons.

Wood-Burned Gourd

A gourd that is free of blemishes can be left unpainted and instead decorated with wood-burned designs to complement its subtle natural color.

Materials

Seasoned birdhouse (or martin) gourd
> (See "Using Gourds" on page 29.)

Soap

Water

Steel wool

Pencil

Wood-burning tool with narrow tip

Paintbrush

Clear acrylic spray

1. Soak the gourd in soapy water for 20 minutes and use the steel wool to scrub off all dirt and mold. Allow the gourd to dry completely.

2. Draw your design on the gourd in pencil, using Figure 1 (see page 90) as a guide.

3. Engrave over the penciled lines with the narrow-tipped wood-burning tool. For dark lines, you will need to engrave over them more than once.

4. Use the paintbrush to apply a coat of clear varnish.

Figure 1

A wood-burned gourd (see page 89), an evergreen swag (see page 92), and a birch log arrangement (see page 126) dress up this handsome rock fireplace.

Evergreen Swag

Sweet-smelling evergreens, chunky pinecones, and plump walnuts—the best of the forest comes inside on this graceful swag.

Materials

8 pinecones, 4 to 6 inches long

20 stems of Fraser fir or other evergreen, 8 inches long

50 stems of cedar, 8 inches long

10 to 15 extra stems of fir and/or cedar, in various lengths

11 walnuts

10 pieces of white annual statice, 3 inches long

Matte white acrylic paint

1-inch flat paintbrush

5 feet of heavy-gauge wire, cut into one 3-foot piece and two 12-inch pieces

Wire cutters

Fine-gauge floral wire

2 yards of white and gold net ribbon, 4 inches wide

2 yards of gold ribbon, 2 inches wide

Hot-glue gun and glue sticks

1. Bake the pinecones at 200°F for 25 minutes to kill any insect eggs or larvae. Allow to cool.

2. Using the white paint and the paintbrush, paint the tips of the pinecone "petals" and set them aside to dry.

3. Use the two pieces of heavy-gauge wire to make two hangers. (See "Making Hangers" on page 22.)

4. Using the fine-gauge wire, wire together two Fraser fir stems and five cedar stems. Repeat the process nine more times, to make a total of ten evergreen bunches. The bunches should be full; add some of the extra pieces of greenery if necessary.

5. Wire the evergreen bunches to the 3-foot piece of heavy-gauge wire, using the fine-gauge wire to attach them. Distribute the bunches evenly along the length of the wire, with the stems pointing in the same direction and the foliage of each bunch covering the stems of the previous one. If there are any holes in the swag when you finish, wire the extra pieces into the openings.

6. Lay the net ribbon along the length of the swag, allowing it to billow up occasionally, and wire it to the swag in three or four places with the fine-gauge wire.

7. Drape the gold ribbon along the swag, positioning it so that it crosses the net ribbon in some spots. Secure it to the swag at the same places where the net ribbon is attached, but form a loop in the ribbon at each juncture.

8. Wire the pinecones to the swag, spacing them attractively among the greenery. (See "Floral Wire" on page 17.)

9. Hot-glue the nuts and statice to the swag, clustering them around the pinecones.

Stuffed Stocking and Package Decorations

A trio of decorations dresses up a corner in need of some Christmas spirit. The green velvet stocking is stuffed with fragrant potpourri, and the packages are dressed in last summer's herbs and flowers.

Pink Foil Package

Materials

11 dried purple annual statice flowers

22 pink globe amaranths

38 yellow santolina flowers

5 pink strawflowers

5 green hops flowers

9 sprigs of pearly everlasting

$4 \times 5\frac{1}{2} \times 7$-inch cardboard box

Sheet of pink foil gift-wrapping paper or florist's foil

5-inch-diameter bowl

Dull knife

Hot-glue gun and glue sticks

Floral fixative spray

1. Wrap the box with the pink foil.

2. Place the bowl in the center of the box and trace around it lightly with the knife, scribing a circle onto the paper.

3. Using the knife to scribe the lines, divide the circle into six vertical sections.

4. Working from left to right, fill in one section of the circle at a time by hot-gluing flowers to completely cover the foil: first the purple statice at far left, then the globe amaranth, the yellow santolina, the strawflowers, the hops, and finally the pearly everlasting at far right.

5. Spray the flowers with floral fixative.

Red Striped Package

Materials

3 hops leaves

1 yarrow bloom, $2\frac{1}{2}$ inches in diameter

1 dried red rose

5 sprigs of baby's-breath, 3 inches long

4 anise hyssop flowers

5 white globe amaranths

1 orange and yellow strawflower

3 hops flowers, stems cut to 4 inches

2 pieces of annual statice

$1\frac{1}{4} \times 5 \times 10$-inch cardboard box

Sheet of red-and-white-striped gift-wrapping paper

1 yard of red velvet ribbon, $1\frac{1}{2}$ inches wide, cut into one 12-inch piece and one 24-inch piece

Hot-glue gun and glue sticks

Floral fixative spray

1. Wrap the box with the gift-wrapping paper.

2. Wrap the longer piece of ribbon around the box lengthwise and hot-glue the ends to the package. Wrap the shorter piece of ribbon around the width of the box and hot-glue the ends to the paper.

3. Hot-glue the hops leaves to the center of the intersecting ribbons with their tips pointing outward.

4. Hot-glue the flowers to the center of the package in the order listed, using the photo as a guide.

5. Spray the flowers with floral fixative.

Stuffed Stocking

Materials

1 cup of potpourri (See page 101 for recipes.)

8 to 10 stems of arborvitae, 10 to 12 inches long

8 stems of yarrow, 8 inches long

6 stems of dried purple annual statice, 7 inches long

6 stems of dried chamomile, 5 to 7 inches long

3 dried yellow roses, 5 to 7 inches long

3 × 5-inch cloth bag with drawstring

Foot-long green velvet stocking with lace trim

3 sheets of tissue paper, 17 × 24 inches

Rubber band

1. Fill the drawstring bag with potpourri and stuff it into the toe of the stocking.

2. Crush the three sheets of tissue paper into balls and stuff them into the stocking, filling it to within 5 inches of the top.

3. Form a bouquet with the greenery, herbs, and flowers and secure their stems with a rubber band.

4. Insert the bouquet into the stocking.

Christmas Horn

Fit for an angel to blow on Christmas morn, this well-decorated craft horn makes a fine door display.

Materials

4 small cones

15 stems of green eucalyptus, ten 14 inches long and five 6 inches long

5 brown and black feathers, 14 inches long (available in craft supply stores)

15 stems of rust eucalyptus, ten 14 inches long and five 6 inches long

12 stems of dried white heather, eight 10 inches long and four 6 inches long

14 stems of green-dyed sweet Annie, ten 8 inches long and four 6 inches long

7 stems of baby's-breath, 8 inches long

Electric drill with ³⁄₁₆-inch bit

8 × 3½ × ¼-inch piece of wood

Chenille craft stem or pipe cleaner

Cool-glue gun and glue sticks

6 × 2 × 1-inch block of floral foam

12-inch craft horn

Floral picks

2 yards of striped ribbon, 1½ inches wide

Scissors

1 yard of ribbon cord with tasseled ends

1. Bake the pinecones at 200°F for 25 minutes to kill any insect eggs or larvae.

2. Drill two holes through the piece of wood, positioning them about 3 inches apart and 1 inch from one of the long edges; the two holes should be roughly centered from side to side. Insert the ends of the chenille stem through the holes, forming a loop. Double the ends back over the edge of the wood and twist the ends around the sides of the loop to form a hanger (see Figure 1).

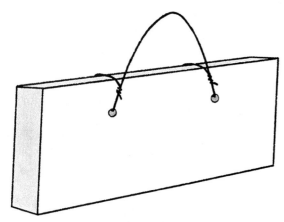

Figure 1

3. Using the cool-glue gun, glue the floral foam to the center of the piece of wood on the side without the hanger.

4. Position the horn with its top curve against the top of the foam block and glue the horn securely to the foam (see Figure 2).

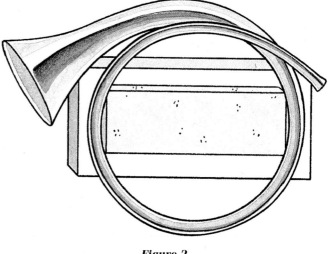

Figure 2

5. Attach floral picks to the stems of all the materials except the cones. (See "Floral Picks" on page 16.)

6. Insert the 14-inch green eucalyptus and the feathers into the floral foam, arranging them in an arch around the top perimeter of the foam. Leave the bottom of the foam free.

7. Pick in the remaining eucalyptus, both rust and green, using the photo as a guide.

8. Tie the ribbon into a multi-loop bow with 12-inch streamers and glue it in place. (See "Making Bows" on page 30.) Trim the streamer ends in inverted V shapes.

9. Fold the ribbon cord in half, twist the wire of a floral pick around the fold, and pick the cord into the foam underneath the bow.

10. Saving the delicate baby's-breath for last, insert the remaining picked materials into the foam, keeping the shorter lengths toward the top center of the arrangement. Glue the pinecones in place around the bow.

Potpourris

Delightfully floral or bracingly evergreen, potpourris are perfect for bedroom or bath. Spoon the potpourri into a decorative basket or bowl and allow it to perfume the air.

Evergreen Potpourri

Materials

For the fixative:

½ cup of orrisroot granules

2 teaspoons of cedar oil

2 teaspoons of tangerine oil

½ teaspoon of clove oil

1-pint glass jar with lid

For the potpourri:

2 cups of pine needles, cut into 1-inch pieces

4 cups of dried incense cedar

1 cup of orange peel pieces

1 cup of lemon peel pieces

2 cups of hemlock cones

1 cup of rose hips

½ cup of cinnamon pieces

2 cups of star anise

2 cups of whole allspice

1½ cups of whole cloves

6-quart plastic container with cover

Long-handled spoon

Floral Potpourri

Materials

For the fixative:

½ cup of orrisroot granules

2 teaspoons of rose oil

1-pint glass jar with lid

For the potpourri:

3 cups of whole old roses

3 cups of rosemary needles

3 cups of lavender flowers

1 cup of hibiscus flowers

3 cups of finely chopped orange peel

6-quart plastic container with cover

Long-handled spoon

1. To prepare the fixative, place the orrisroot granules and essential oils in the glass jar. Cover the jar and shake well to mix. Set aside for five days, shaking daily.

2. When the fixative is ready, place the herbs, spices, and flowers in the plastic container in the order listed, stirring after each addition with the long-handled spoon.

3. Add the fixative to the potpourri mixture and stir well. Store potpourri in the covered plastic container.

4. Display the potpourri in a basket, glass, or pottery bowl. Avoid metal containers, which may cause the essential oils to become rancid.

Driftwood Santas

*If you've ever strolled along an ocean beach or the shore of one
of the Great Lakes, you've probably picked up an interesting piece
of driftwood, carried it for half a mile, and then tossed it aside
when you could think of nothing to do with it. You can put that
chunk of wood to good use creating Santas that welcome guests
from your front porch or stand sentry by the Christmas tree.*

Materials

  Piece of driftwood

  Handsaw

  Acrylic paints

  Paintbrushes

  Clear varnish spray

1. Check to see that the driftwood will stand upright. If it won't, use the handsaw to slice off a portion of it to produce a level bottom.

2. Brush off any sand or dirt from the driftwood and allow it to dry out for several days.

3. Paint the driftwood with acrylic paints in the colors of your choice. Depending on the wood's shape, the entire piece can be painted as a single Santa, or several figures can project from the wood. You may want to use the photos for inspiration or Figures 1 and 2 (see page 104) and Figure 3 (see page 105) as guides.

4. When the paint is completely dry, spray the entire piece with clear varnish.

Figure 1

Figure 2

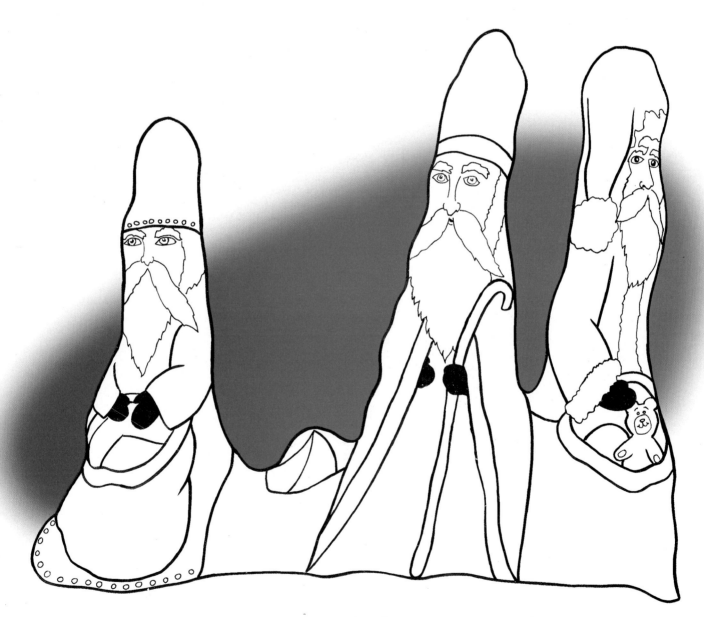

Figure 3

Fragrant Tussie Mussie

Bee balm and evergreens add delicate fragrance to this colorful tussie mussie. If you pack the tussie mussie in protective tissue paper and store it in a dark place, it will still look lovely the following Christmas—you'll just need to replace the old evergreens with fresh-cut ones.

Materials

9 stems of dried bee balm, 6 inches long, with foliage still attached

8 stems of dried yarrow, 6 inches long

6 stems of pepperberries or silk berries, 4 inches long

10 stems of fresh-cut evergreens, 4 inches long

7 stems of dried baby's-breath, 4 inches long

7-inch-diameter cotton crocheted doily

Fabric stiffener

Floral tape

1. Arrange the stems of bee balm and yarrow into a loose bouquet and set it aside.

2. Cut a 1-inch hole out of the center of the doily and treat it with fabric stiffener, according to the manufacturer's instructions.

3. Gently push the stems of the bouquet down through the hole, allowing them to protrude about 2 inches and keeping the bouquet loose enough to allow space for the remaining materials.

4. Shape the doily around the outer edges of the bouquet and allow it to dry completely before beginning the next step.

5. Carefully insert the remainder of the materials down into the base of the bouquet, working first with the berries, then the evergreens, then the delicate baby's-breath. Securely wrap the protruding stems with floral tape.

Moss Tree

With its garland of leaves and flowers, this restrained but handsome moss-covered tree would make a fine addition to a den or master bedroom.

Materials

    2 square feet of garden moss

    20 dark pink strawflowers

    20 cockscomb heads, 1½ inches in diameter

    20 sprigs of pepperberries, 1½ inches in diameter

    20 lamb's-ears

    20 nigella pods

    20 sprigs of dried larkspur, 1 inch long

    20 dried feverfew flowers

    20 bay leaves

    20 sprigs of 'Silver King' artemisia, 2 to 3 inches long

    20 cinnamon sticks

    Hot-glue gun and glue sticks

    1 grapevine tree, 13 inches high

    3 yards of ribbon, ¼ inch wide

1. Hot-glue the moss to the grapevine tree, covering the tree completely.

2. To create a design line to follow, hot-glue one end of the ribbon at the base of the tree. Wind the ribbon around the tree in a spiral, working from bottom to top and holding the ribbon in place every few inches with a dab of hot glue.

3. Using the ribbon as a guide, hot-glue the flowers, leaves, and pods to the ribbon and the adjacent moss in a spiral pattern, starting at the bottom of the tree and ending at the top. Arrange the materials randomly, varying colors, textures, and shapes.

Kissing Ball

Any enterprising person can arrange a kiss at Christmastime whether there's mistletoe around or not. If you happen to have a sprig, place it inside this colorful kissing ball. If you have none at the moment, hang the kissing ball in a doorway, and inform your sweetheart that tradition demands one kiss for each globe amaranth.

Materials

    31 mountain mint leaves

    31 lunaria seedpods

    31 red globe amaranths

    Purchased grapevine ball, 8 inches in diameter

    Hot-glue gun and glue sticks

    3¼ yards of white grosgrain ribbon, ¼ inch wide, cut into one 46-inch piece, four 15-inch pieces, and one 7-inch piece

    Scissors

1. Visually divide the grapevine ball into vertical thirds. Starting at the top of the ball in one section, hot-glue ten mountain mint leaves onto the grapevine ball in a spiral, moving from the top right to the bottom left, with the top of each leaf touching the stem of the previous one.

2. Move one-third of the way around the circumference of the ball and make a second spiral of mint leaves. Move another one-third and make a third spiral, this time using 11 leaves.

3. Hot-glue a lunaria seedpod to each mint leaf, positioning it slightly to the right.

4. Hot-glue one globe amaranth to the base of each seedpod.

5. To form a hanger, loop the 46-inch piece of ribbon through the top of the kissing ball and tie the ends together.

6. To make the streamers, thread the four 15-inch pieces of ribbon through the bottom of the ball—two going one way and two going perpendicular to the first pair. Gather all four ribbons close to the ball, and tie them together with the 7-inch piece of ribbon. Trim the ends of the 7-inch piece, and trim each streamer with an angled cut.

Cedar and Pepperberry Swag

Abundant with blooming flowers and ripened berries, this curved swag will drape beautifully over a mirror or a favorite picture.

Materials

12 stems of cedar, 12 inches long

8 stems of boxwood, 10 inches long

12 stems of German statice, 6 to 8 inches long

2 heads of cockscomb, 3 inches in diameter

2 stems of pepperberries, 5 inches long

Wire cutters

Wire coat hanger

Green floral tape

Medium-gauge floral wire

2 yards of green velvet ribbon, 2 inches wide

Fine-gauge floral wire

Hot-glue gun and glue sticks

1. Using the wire cutters, clip off the bottom of the wire coat hanger (see Figure 1) and bend it into an arch. Bend the hook down to serve as a hanger for the finished swag.

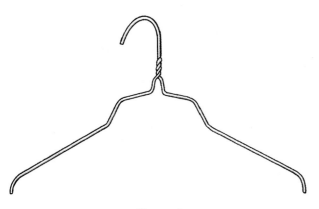

Figure 1

2. Wrap floral tape around the wire base, covering it completely.

3. Using the medium-gauge floral wire, wire six cedar stems to the center of the arch, with their tips pointing to the left. Wire the remaining six cedar stems to the center with their tips pointing to the right.

4. Wire four stems of boxwood to the left of the swag and four to the right.

5. Make a bow from the green velvet ribbon (see "Making Bows" on page 30) and wire the bow around its center with the fine-gauge floral wire. Attach the bow to the center of the swag with the medium-gauge wire.

6. Hot-glue the German statice on both sides of the swag, with all stem ends pointing toward the center.

7. Hot-glue one cockscomb head on each side of the bow.

8. Hot-glue a stem of pepperberries next to each cockscomb head.

Guest Room Decorations

When family and friends fill your house for the holidays, it's fun to add a few festive touches to the guest bedrooms. A floral topiary will delight any visiting gardeners, while a cheery birdhouse will please your bird-watching guests.

Topiary

Materials

4-inch-diameter clump of Spanish moss

1 cinnamon stick, 12 inches long

3 magnolia leaves

6 poppy pods

5 dried pink roses

12 sprigs of Fraser fir, 3 to 4 inches long

6 clusters of pepperberries, 3 inches in diameter

2 clumps of dried lichen, about 2 inches in diameter

15 pieces of plumosa fern, 3 inches long

Hot-glue gun and glue sticks

3 × 3 × 4-inch block of floral foam

4-inch-diameter basket, 3 inches tall

Floral pins

2 × 2 × 2-inch block of floral foam

60 inches of lace ribbon, 1½ inches wide, cut into one 56-inch-long piece and one 4-inch-long piece

Fine-gauge floral wire

1. Hot-glue the 3 × 3 × 4-inch block of foam into the bottom of the basket. Cover the foam with the Spanish moss, securing the moss with floral pins.

2. Insert the cinnamon stick into the foam and hot-glue around the juncture of the foam and the cinnamon stick.

3. Hot-glue the 2 × 2 × 2-inch block of foam to the top of the cinnamon stick.

4. Make a five-loop bow with the lace ribbon, making one 6-inch streamer and one 22-inch streamer. (See "Making Bows" on page 30.) Wire the bow at its center and pin it into the top foam block with floral pins.

5. Wind the 22-inch streamer loosely around the cinnamon stick and pin it into the bottom block of foam. Bring the streamer over the edge of the basket and down the outside, and hot-glue it to the side of the basket at the very bottom. Stretch the remaining length of ribbon out on the table, perpendicular to the basket.

6. Insert two magnolia leaves into the foam base and hot-glue the third on top of the piece of ribbon on the table.

7. Hot-glue the 4-inch piece of ribbon on top of the magnolia leaf on the table.

8. Hot-glue three poppy pods to the top arrangement, two to the bottom arrangement, and one to the table arrangement.

9. Hot-glue two roses to the top of the arrangement and three to the bottom arrangement.

10. Hot-glue four sprigs of Fraser fir to the top arrangement, six to the bottom arrangement, and two to the table arrangement.

11. Hot-glue two clusters of pepperberries to the top arrangement, three to the bottom arrangement, and one to the table arrangement.

12. Hot-glue the lichen to the basket.

13. Hot-glue the fern pieces to the arrangement, dividing them among the three locations.

Birdhouse

Materials

- Small handful of Spanish moss
- 3 preserved oak leaves
- 8 birch twigs, 8 inches long
- 9 pieces of pink ti tree, three 8 inches long and six 4 inches long
- 6 sprays of green peppergrass, 6 inches long
- 4 clusters of pepperberries, 3 inches in diameter
- 10 pieces of ming fern, six 6 inches long and four 3 inches long
- 2 clumps of dried lichen, 2 inches in diameter
- Purchased bark birdhouse, 6½ inches tall and 3 inches in diameter
- 4 × 4 × ¾-inch block of floral foam
- Felt-tipped marker
- Serrated knife
- Hot-glue gun and glue sticks
- Floral pins
- 1 × 1 × ¾-inch block of floral foam
- 2 artificial birds, about 2 to 3 inches long from beak to tail
- Medium-gauge floral wire

1. Set the birdhouse in the center of the 4 × 4-inch block of floral foam and trace around the bottom of the birdhouse with the felt-tipped marker. Using the serrated knife, cut out the circle you have traced.

2. Hot-glue the circle of foam to the bottom of the birdhouse. The sides and the bottom of the foam circle will serve as points of attachment for twigs, foliage, and berries.

3. Arrange the Spanish moss around the circumference of the foam circle, securing it with floral pins.

4. Hot-glue the three oak leaves to the bottom of the foam circle, so that they cover the foam completely and protrude out from the circle on both sides.

5. Hot-glue the 1-inch-square piece of foam to one side of the roof, near the peak.

6. Hot-glue one bird to the foam block on top of the house. Wire the other bird's feet around the perch on the birdhouse. If there is no perch, hot-glue the bird to the front of the house. Use the photo as a guide for positioning.

7. In the order listed, hot-glue the birch twigs, ti tree, peppergrass, pepperberries, and ming fern to the two pieces of foam, dividing the materials between the roof and the base. Hot-glue one clump of dried lichen into the roof arrangement and the other to the opposite side of the roof.

Scented Bath Decorations

To dress up a guest bath for the holidays, place a colorful bottle of herbal bath fragrance next to the tub and a pretty jar of potpourri on the vanity.

Rosemary Bath Fragrance

Materials

3 cups of freshly cut rosemary sprigs plus 4 to 6 sprigs for garnish

Heat-proof 1-quart jar

Boiling water

Strainer

Measuring cup

Large bowl

Measuring spoons

About 4½ teaspoons of grain alcohol

Decorative bottles with caps or stoppers

Food coloring

Hot-glue gun and glue sticks

1 yard of lace ribbon, ½ inch wide

½ yard of gold craft beads

1. Place the cut rosemary in the quart jar. Add boiling water to fill the jar and allow the liquid to cool.

2. Pour the cooled liquid through a strainer into a measuring cup until the cup is full; transfer the measured liquid into a large bowl. Continue the process until you have emptied the liquid into the bowl, keeping track of how much liquid you have.

3. For each cup of liquid, add 1⅛ teaspoons of grain alcohol and stir.

4. Pour the liquid into decorative bottles. Place the reserved sprigs of fresh rosemary in the bottles and add food coloring a drop at a time until you are pleased with the color.

5. Hot-glue the center of the ribbon to the center back of the bottle's neck, then hot-glue the ribbon around the rest of the neck. Tie the ends in a bow.

6. Wrap the gold beads around the neck of the bottle and tie them in a bow.

Potpourri Jar

Materials

2 cups of dried roses and rose petals

5 to 7 Queen-Anne's-lace blooms

5 to 7 carnations

3 to 5 small clumps of garden moss

2 sprigs of silk berries, 3 inches long

2 stems of Fraser fir, or other fragrant evergreen, 3 inches long

Decorative jar with lid

Rose-scented essential oil

Hot-glue gun and glue sticks

18 inches of lace ribbon, ½ inch wide

1. Mix the roses and petals, the Queen-Anne's-lace, the carnations, and the moss in the decorative jar, reserving one attractive rose for decoration.

2. Add essential oil one drop at a time until you reach the desired fragrance. Place the lid on the jar and shake the ingredients gently to disperse the oil.

3. Hot-glue the center of the ribbon to the back of the jar's neck. Glue the ribbon all the way around the neck, then tie it in a bow. Hot-glue a spray of berries and a stem of fir on each side of the bow, then hot-glue the reserved rose into the center of the bow, taking care to cover all stems.

4. If the jar has a hollow lid with a removable plastic stopper that fits inside the lid, fill the lid with potpourri as well.

Dress up a quest room for the holidays with a topiary
(see page 112) and birdhouse (see page 114),
scented bath decorations (see page 116),
a flower and leaf garland (see page 120),
and decorated sachets (see page 134).

Flower and Leaf Garland

Lush with herbs and flowers, this colorful garland will drape beautifully along a mantel, over a window or door, or around the bedposts.

Materials

65 spruce cones

6 full stems of peeled lunaria, giving
    64 seedpods

64 bay leaves

64 heads of cockscomb, 1 to 1½ inches long

64 pink and white globe amaranths

64 strawflowers, in assorted colors

#18 tapestry needle

13 feet of monofilament fishing line

1. Bake the spruce cones at 200°F for 25 minutes to kill any insect eggs or larvae.

2. Thread the needle with the monofilament fishing line.

3. Cut the lunaria off the stems, leaving no stems remaining on the pods.

4. Thread the flowers, cones, and leaves onto the monofilament in the following order: one spruce cone, one bay leaf, one cockscomb head, one globe amaranth, one lunaria pod, and one strawflower.

5. Following the same order, continue threading until all materials have been used. As you arrange the materials, leave 6 inches of monofilament bare at each end.

6. Thread a spruce cone onto the other end of the monofilament and tie a knot at each end.

Gourd Christmas Tree

With its bright primary colors and shiny surface, this light-hearted table tree is perfect for a child's room. The tree in the photo stands about 14 inches tall, but the height will vary depending on the size of your gourds. From its shining star to its Christmas lights to its gold garlands, the tree is made entirely from gourds.

Materials

4 seasoned teardrop-shaped martin gourds in graduated sizes (See "Using Gourds" on page 29.)

14-inch piece of seasoned dipper-gourd handle

200 gourd seeds

6 × 8-inch bunch of dried fibrous pith from a loofah gourd

Soap

Water

Steel wool

Sharp craft knife

Coping saw

Green spray enamel

Gold spray paint

Brown, red, and white acrylic paints

Paintbrush

Metallic paints

White craft glue

Wood putty

Scissors

Figure 1

1. Soak the gourds in soapy water for 20 minutes and use the steel wool to scrub off all dirt and mold. Allow to dry completely.

2. Using the end of the sharp craft knife to start the cuts and the coping saw to complete them, cut the four martin gourds as shown in Figures 1, 2, 3, and 4. The shaded areas represent the gourd pieces that will be used for the tree branches. Check to be sure that the four pieces stack reasonably well.

3. From a leftover gourd piece, cut a star for the top of the tree.

4. To make the tree stand, select one of the gourd tops left over from cutting the tree branch pieces. Cut off the top of this piece (see Figure 5). Check to see that the bottom is level, and trim if necessary.

5. Insert the dipper gourd handle into the tree stand and stack the tree pieces on top.

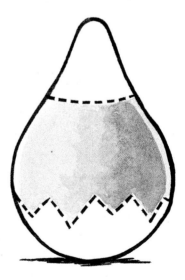

Figure 2

Check to see whether the "trunk" is the right length. If it's too long, cut off the dipper handle to the desired length.

6. Spray the four tree pieces, inside and out, with the green enamel and allow them to dry. Spray the star gold. Paint the piece of dipper-gourd handle brown. Paint the tree stand red and white.

7. Paint one side of the seeds in a variety of colors, using the metallic paint.

8. Glue the tree pieces together, with the largest on the bottom and the smallest on top.

9. Insert the trunk into the tree stand and, using the white craft glue, glue the two pieces together. Fill in any gaps with wood putty. Allow to dry.

10. Insert the trunk into the bottom of the tree and glue it in place, filling any gaps with wood putty. Allow to dry.

11. Glue the colored seeds randomly around the tree to represent lights, then glue the star to the top of the tree.

12. Use the scissors to cut the outer fibrous layer off the loofah. Cut that layer into strips about ½ inch wide. Spray the strips with gold paint and allow them to dry. Glue the strips onto the tree, fitting them together end to end and draping them as if they were garlands.

Figure 3

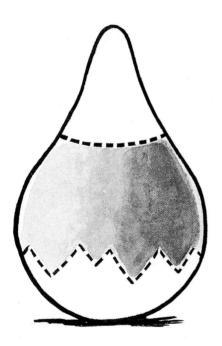

Figure 4

Figure 5

Red and White Floral Wreath

Here's a Christmas wreath in traditional red and white with a golden bow accent.

Materials

- 3 large handfuls of Spanish moss
- 20 stems of cedar, 6 inches long
- 10 stems of boxwood, 4 inches long
- 12 sprigs of German statice, 3 inches long
- 4 heads of cockscomb, 2 inches in diameter
- 10 sprigs of pepperberries, 2 inches long
- 8 dried red roses
- 10 sprigs of white annual statice, 2 inches long
- 8 red strawflowers
- 10-inch single-wire wreath base
- Monofilament fishing line
- Scissors
- Hot-glue gun and glue sticks
- 3 yards of red-and-gold-paisley satin ribbon, 2½ inches wide
- Fine-gauge floral wire

1. Hold a handful of Spanish moss against the wire wreath base and wrap the monofilament fishing line around both moss and base in a spiral fashion. Continue adding moss and wrapping with monofilament until the base is covered. Wrap the monofilament around the base a final time, tie it in a knot, and trim the end with the scissors.

2. Hot-glue the cedar stems around the base with their tips all pointing in the same direction. Hot-glue the boxwood stems around the wreath in the same fashion.

3. Hot-glue the flowers and berries to the greenery in the order listed, distributing them evenly around the wreath.

4. Form the paisley ribbon into a bow with 20-inch streamers, and wire the bow together at its center, leaving wire ends about 8 inches long. (See "Making Bows" on page 30.) Use the wire ends to attach the bow to the top of the wreath. Cut the streamer ends on the diagonal, making them slightly uneven in length.

Birch Log Arrangement

*Loveliest of trees, the birch is instantly recogniz-
able by its wintery white bark. A fallen branch can
be retrieved from the forest floor and hung with
blooms for a handsome table arrangement.*

Materials

20-inch-long birch log

Small handful of Spanish moss

16 sprigs of boxwood, two 10 inches long, six 6 inches long, and eight 3 inches long

9 sprigs of ti tree, five 9 inches long and four 6 inches long

20 sprigs of white larkspur, 6 inches long

10 dried red roses, three 7 inches long, five 5 inches long, and two 3 inches long

5 sprigs of preserved green fern, 6 to 8 inches long

8 pieces of white annual statice, 4 inches long

Hot-glue gun and glue sticks

1½ × 1½ × 1-inch block of floral foam

1½ yards of red plaid ribbon, 1 inch wide

Medium-gauge floral wire

Heavy-duty scissors

1. Hot-glue the block of floral foam to the center of the log, positioning the block so that it is 1½ inches long and wide and 1 inch high.

2. Lay the Spanish moss over the foam, covering it completely. Hot-glue the moss in place at several points.

3. Set aside three of the 3-inch sprigs of boxwood and insert the remaining sprigs into the floral foam in an oval pattern, following the shape of the log, hot-gluing them in place. Start with the two long pieces, positioning them on opposite sides of the bow and laying them along the length of the log. Arrange the 6-inch pieces next in an oval, and then add the five 3-inch pieces.

4. Hot-glue the remaining materials to the arrangement, distributing them evenly: first the ti tree, then the larkspur, the roses, the fern, and ending with the statice.

5. Make a bow with the ribbon and wire the bow at its center with the floral wire. (See "Making Bows" on page 30.) Use the scissors to trim the wire ends to 4 inches.

6. Insert the bow's wire ends into the foam. Hot-glue the bow in place at two or three strategic points.

7. Place a dab of hot glue on the end of a reserved boxwood sprig and insert it into the arrangement through the loops of the bow. Repeat this procedure with the other reserved sprigs.

Maple Pod Wreath

In the fall, the seedpods of maple trees spin dizzily to the ground, more aerodynamically adept than Wilbur and Orville ever hoped to be. In December, the same seedpods can decorate a handsome wreath that's sure to be a conversation piece.

Materials

100 to 130 maple seedpods

3 pieces of ming fern, 4 to 6 inches long

Wire cutters

Medium-gauge floral wire

10-inch-diameter plywood wreath base

Hot-glue gun and glue sticks

2½ yards of red velvet ribbon, ¾ inch wide, cut into one 1-yard piece and one 1½-yard piece

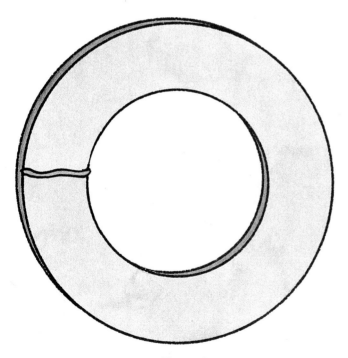

Figure 1

1. To make a hanger, cut a 12-inch piece of wire and twist it in the center to form a loop with two long ends. Wrap the wire ends around one side of the wreath base, with one wire on each side of the base, and twist the wire ends together. Tuck the wire ends to the back side of the base. (See "Making Hangers" on page 22.)

2. Place a bead of hot glue across the wreath base and hot-glue a row of seedpods to the base (see Figure 1). Hot-glue a second row of seedpods in a similar fashion, overlapping the stems of the first row with the tips of the second. Continue around the base until it is entirely covered with rows of seedpods.

3. Form a loop in the center of the 1-yard piece of ribbon and hot-glue it together where the two sides cross. Hot-glue the ribbon loop near the top of the wreath.

4. Make a tailored bow and hot-glue it to the ribbon loop. (See "Making Bows" on page 30.)

5. Hot-glue the fern into the bow, tucking the stems in, using the photo as a guide.

Gourd Wise Men

These two plump gourds paint a wonderful picture of the men who came to see Christ: wise enough not to miss a good dinner, affable enough to buy presents, and generous enough to give them away.

Materials

2 seasoned pear-shaped gourds
  (See "Using Gourds" on page 29.)

Soap

Water

Steel wool

Pencil

Acrylic paints in assorted colors

1-inch flat paintbrush

Paintbrush with pointed tip

Black permanent marker with fine tip

Clear acrylic spray

1. Soak the gourds in soapy water for 20 minutes and use the steel wool to scrub off all dirt and mold. Allow to dry completely.

2. Sketch your design on the gourds in pencil, using Figure 1 (see page 132) and Figure 2 (see page 133) as patterns.

3. Using the photo as a guide, paint the gourds in the desired colors, using one color at a time and allowing each color to dry before proceeding with the next.

4. Use the permanent marker to outline any features you want to clearly define, such as the eyes and eyelashes.

5. After all the paint is completely dry, spray the painted gourds with the clear acrylic spray.

Figure 1

Figure 2

Decorated Sachets

*A pretty, sweet-smelling sachet decorated
with leaves and flowers will delight every aunt,
mother, and grandmother on your gift list.*

Materials

For the sachet at left:

1 pink strawflower

2 sprigs of artemisia

2 dried cockscomb heads

6 × 22-inch piece of mauve moire fabric

1½ cups of homemade or purchased potpourri
(See page 101 for potpourri recipes.)

½ yard of rose ribbon, ⅛ inch wide

Needle and thread

Iron

Hot-glue gun and glue sticks

For the center sachet:

3 sprigs of preserved cedar, 6 inches long

3 sprigs of pepperberries, 2 inches long

1 white strawflower

6 × 22-inch piece of dark green fabric

1½ cups of homemade or purchased potpourri

½ yard of plaid ribbon, ½ inch wide

Needle and thread

Iron

Hot-glue gun and glue sticks

For the sachet at right:

3 sprigs of baby's-breath, 1 inch long

2 dried cockscomb heads

1 dried red rose

1 white strawflower

6 × 22-inch piece of red-and-white patterned
fabric

1½ cups of homemade or purchased potpourri

½ yard of white satin ribbon, ⅛ inch wide

Needle and thread

Iron

Hot-glue gun and glue sticks

1. For each sachet, fold the fabric in half, right
sides together, to form a vertical rectangle. Sew
the side and bottom seams and turn the bag
right-side-out. Fold the top down inside the bag
2 inches and press with a hot iron. Fill the cloth
bag with the potpourri and tie it closed with the
ribbon. Tie the ribbon ends into a simple bow.

2. Begin decorating the sachet by positioning
the stems of the longest material at the center of
the bow with all stems pointing toward the center
of the arrangement, then hot-glue the stems in
place. Layer on any additional stems and hot-glue
them in place. Arrange single blooms to cover the
area where the stems meet, and hot-glue.

Creche with Christmas Herbs

Christmas legends surround various herbs. For example, pennyroyal supposedly bloomed at midnight on the first Christmas Eve, lavender gained its fine fragrance when Mary laid her newly washed cloak on the plant to dry, and thyme filled the manger where the baby lay. Legends aside, herbs make fine decorations for a purchased creche.

Materials

4 square feet of garden moss

24-inch-long piece of ivy

4 stems of pine, 8 inches long

4 stems of pennyroyal, 6 inches long

3 stems of horehound, 6 inches long

2 stems of rue, 6 inches long

2 stems of our-lady's bedstraw, 6 inches long

3 stems of yarrow, 6 inches long

3 stems of lavender, 2 inches long

15 stems of globe amaranth, 6 inches long

4 sprigs of rosemary, 6 inches long

4 stems of cedar, 7 inches long

2 sprigs of chamomile, 6 inches long

1 sprig of tansy flowers, 5 inches long

Purchased wooden créche, 1 foot high and 2 feet wide at the base

Hot-glue gun and glue sticks

Fine-gauge floral wire

Creche figurines of your choice

1. Cover the roof and the base of the creche with garden moss, attaching it with dabs of hot glue as necessary.

2. Run the ivy along the front of the roofline, hot-gluing as necessary.

3. Stand the pine stems up against the creche columns and wire them to the columns using the fine-gauge floral wire.

4. In similar fashion, wire the pennyroyal, horehound, rue, and our-lady's bedstraw upright against the columns.

5. Position the creche figures as desired.

6. Tuck the remaining herbs around the creche figures, varying the colors and textures.

Christmas Simmers

Create a scented Christmas with these fragrant simmers. The Citrus Spice Simmer perfumes the house with lemon, orange, and allspice. The Evergreen Herb Simmer combines the clean scents of pine and rosemary with the exotic aromas of coriander and cloves.

Citrus Spice Simmer

Materials

For the fixative:

½ cup of orrisroot granules

25 drops of orange oil

25 drops of cinnamon oil

15 drops of lemon oil

20 drops of clove oil

½-pint glass jar with lid

For the simmer:

2 cups of cinnamon-stick pieces

2 cups of dried orange peel strips

2 cups of whole star anise

1 cup of lemon grass, chopped

1 cup of lemon verbena, chopped

2 cups of dried lemon peel strips

½ cup of whole allspice

½ cup of red juniper berries

½ cup of whole cloves

½ cup of pinquica leaves

½ cup of sandalwood chips

1 cup of yellow chrysanthemum petals

2 cups of tilia flowers

½ cup of sassafras chips

2-gallon plastic container with tight-fitting lid (a plastic trash can works well)

Long-handled spoon

Evergreen Herb Simmer

Materials

For the fixative:

½ cup of orrisroot granules

15 drops of cinnamon oil

7 drops of clove oil

20 drops of cedar oil

10 drops of orange oil

½-pint glass jar with lid

For the simmer:

1 cup of cinnamon-stick pieces

1 cup of whole allspice

2 cups of dried orange peel strips

1 cup of mint leaves, chopped

1 cup of bay leaves, chopped

1 cup of whole coriander

½ cup of rosemary needles

½ cup of chopped pine needles

½ cup of star anise, halved or quartered

½ cup of whole cloves

½ cup of rose hips

2-gallon plastic container with tight-fitting lid (a plastic trash can works well)

Long-handled spoon

1. To prepare the fixative, place the orrisroot granules and essential oils in the glass jar. Cover the jar and shake well to mix. Set aside for five days, shaking daily.

2. When the fixative is ready, place the herbs, spices, and flowers in the plastic container in the order listed, stirring after each addition with the long-handled spoon.

3. Add the fixative to the simmer mixture and stir well. Store the simmer covered.

4. To use, add ½ cup of the simmer to 6 cups of water in a large cooking pot. Bring it to a boil, reduce the heat, and allow the mixture to simmer, adding water as needed to prevent the simmer from boiling dry.

Pinecone Angel

*Place this little angel out of harm's way in
a child's room to inspire angelic behavior
as the holidays draw near.*

Materials

1 pinecone, 4 to 5 inches long

1 sweet gum seedpod

5 longleaf pine needle clusters, caps on

Pruning shears

Clear acrylic spray

Hot-glue gun and glue sticks

Large pot or heat-proof bowl, optional

Boiling water, optional

Fine-gauge floral wire

Wire cutters

14 inches of red satin ribbon, $\frac{1}{16}$ inch
wide, cut into one 3-inch piece
and one 11-inch piece

3-inch-diameter cork disk, such as a
coaster, about $\frac{1}{16}$ inch thick

1. Bake the cone and sweet gum seedpod
at 200°F for 25 minutes to kill any insect eggs
or larvae.

2. Cut off the tip and the stem of the
pinecone with the pruning shears.

3. Spray the cone and seedpod with clear
acrylic and allow them to dry completely.

4. To make the angel's head, hot-glue the
seedpod to the wide end of the cone.

5. If the pine needles are very brittle, put
them in the pot or heat-proof bowl and cover
them with boiling water. Let them soak for
30 minutes.

6. To make the halo, take one pine needle
cluster, divide the needles into three equal
parts, and braid them, securing the end with

a piece of fine-gauge floral wire. Bend the
braid into a circle and, leaving about $\frac{1}{2}$ inch
of each end free, wrap the ends together
with the wire, forming a stand for the halo
(see Figure 1). Trim the ends evenly with the
wire cutters. Bend the stand down at a right
angle to the halo and hot-glue the stand to
the angel's head.

Figure 1

7. To make the wing tips, hold two needle clusters side by side and bend them at a sharp right angle about 4 inches from the caps (see Figure 2). Wire the loose needle ends together. Repeat the procedure with the other two needle clusters.

8. Wire the wing tips together (see Figure 3). Spray them with clear acrylic and set them aside to dry.

9. Halfway down the back of the cone, cut off one or two petals with the pruning shears. Hot-glue the wings into the cavity created by the missing petals. Hot-glue one of the cutoff petals over the wired portion of the wings.

10. Form a two-loop bow with the 3-inch piece of ribbon and hot-glue it to the front of the angel's neck.

11. Hot-glue the remaining ribbon around the front edge of the cork disk and glue the angel to the center of the disk.

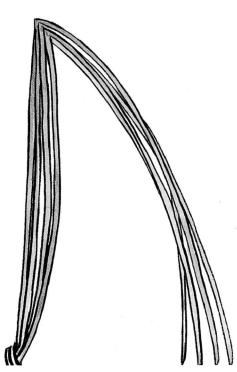

Figure 2

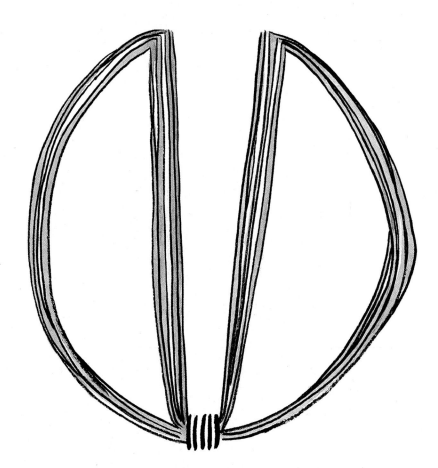

Figure 3

Magnolia Swag

Swirls of grapevine echo loops of copper foil ribbon in this arresting arrangement. If the grapevine is dry and stiff, soak it in a bucket of water overnight to make it pliable.

Materials

11 feet, 4 inches of pliable grapevine, cut into two 28-inch pieces, two 22-inch pieces, and two 18-inch pieces

11 magnolia leaves, 9 large and 2 small

4-inch-diameter clump of physocarpus, cut into 5 small pieces

7 clusters of dried red starflowers, 1 to 2 inches in diameter

2½-inch cube of floral foam

Medium-gauge floral wire

Hot-glue gun and glue sticks

6 strands of raffia, 2 yards long

Wire cutters

Floral picks

2 yards of twisted copper foil ribbon, cut into six 12-inch pieces

1. Insert the end of any grapevine piece into one side of the floral foam. Shape the vine into a large loop and insert the other end into the opposite side of the foam (see Figure 1).

2. Follow the same procedure for a second piece of grapevine (see Figure 2).

3. Repeat Step 1 four more times, until all grapevine pieces are inserted. While the arrangement of the loops can vary, all the large loops should not be on one side or the arrangement will look unbalanced.

4. To make a hanger, cut an 8-inch piece of the floral wire and bend it into a loop, leaving a 1-inch tail of twisted wire. Put a dab of hot glue on the end of the wire and insert it into the foam. (See "Making Hangers" on page 22.)

5. Make a bow (see "Making Bows" on page 30) with the six strands of raffia and wire the

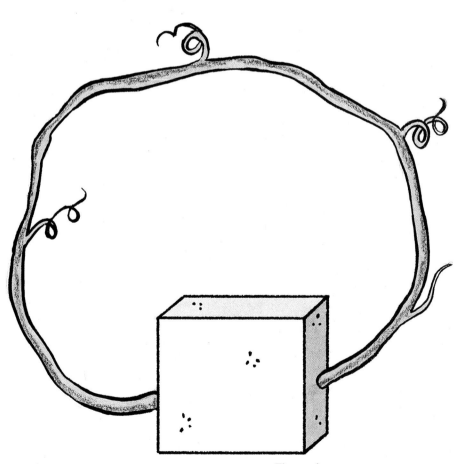

Figure 1

bow at its center. Cut off the wire ends, leaving a tail of twisted wire about 1 inch long. Insert the wire tail into the front of the foam, adding dabs of hot glue as necessary to hold the bow in place.

6. Wire the magnolia leaves to floral picks. Pick the nine large leaves around the circumference of the foam, arranging them in a sunburst pattern. Pick the two small leaves into the center of the bow. (See "Floral Picks" on page 16.)

7. Wire the five pieces of physocarpus to floral picks and pick them randomly into the arrangement.

8. Form the pieces of copper foil into loops and wire each one to a floral pick. Pick the loops into the arrangement.

9. Wire the clusters of starflowers to floral picks and pick them randomly around the arrangement.

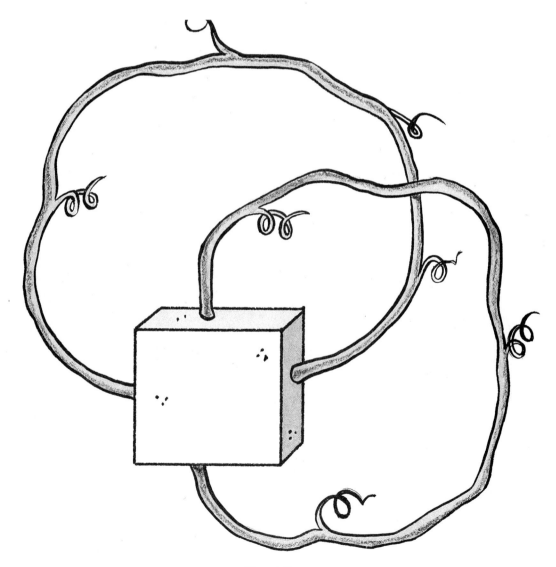

Figure 2

Evergreen and Birch Bark Wreath

With its red pomegranates, white birch bark, brown cones, and dark green foliage, this wreath offers marvelous contrasts in color and texture. The ribbon and vine that wrap around the entire wreath unify the elements in one harmonious circle.

Materials

- 11 medium-sized pinecones
- 80 to 90 stems of fresh evergreens, trimmed to 7 inches
- 45- to 60-inch length of fresh-cut grapevine
- 6 to 8 strips of white birch bark, 4 inches long and 1 to 2 inches wide
- 3 pomegranates
- 6 stems of silk berries, 4 inches long
- 12 stems dried caspia, 6 inches long
- Floral picks
- 26-inch straw wreath base
- Pruning shears
- 1 yard of red plaid ribbon, 1 inch wide
- Hot-glue gun and glue sticks

1. Bake the pinecones at 200°F for 25 minutes to kill any insect eggs or larvae.

2. Strip the needles from the lower 2 inches of the evergreen stems. Arrange the stems in groups of three and attach each group to a floral pick. Pick the greenery into the straw wreath base, with the evergreen bunches facing the same direction. Hide the picked end of each bunch under the greens of the next bunch, covering the wreath base completely in this way.

3. With the pruning shears, cut one end of the vine at a sharp angle and attach that end to a floral pick. Insert the pick into the base and coil the remaining length of vine on the front of the wreath several times, securing the end by tucking it back into the vine.

4. Loosely weave the ribbon around the wreath, placing it under the greenery and the vine in some areas and securing it with a dab of hot glue as needed.

5. Tuck the pieces of birch bark under the vine and ribbon, distributing the pieces evenly around the wreath and holding them in place with a dab of hot glue as necessary.

6. Hot-glue the pomegranates to the greenery, spacing them evenly around the wreath. Hot-glue the berry stems and the caspia to the wreath in the same fashion.

7. Hot-glue the cones around the wreath, positioning them at various angles and depths in the greenery.

❧ Oh Christmas Tree! ❧

Perhaps the most joyous
tradition of the season, the
Christmas tree is nature brought
indoors for the holidays. The
fragrance of cedar, fir, or pine,
the rich green hues that brighten
a room on a gray winter's day,
the well-loved decorations
hanging from the branches, the
presents beneath the tree—all
persuade us to lavish our
Christmas crafting
on ornaments for the tree.

Pinecone Bird Nest

According to Scandinavian legend, each bird's nest in your Christmas tree will bring you a year of good luck. If the nests are especially comfortable, perhaps the good fortune will be abundant. So be sure to select very roomy pinecones for these ornaments.

Materials

For one nest:

5-inch-diameter pinecone, 10 inches long

Large handful of Spanish moss

Pruning shears

Acrylic spray

Scissors

Hot-glue gun and glue sticks

12-inch piece of medium-gauge floral wire

Awl or electric drill with $\frac{1}{16}$-inch bit

Artificial bird, about 3 inches long from beak to tail

1. Bake the pinecone at 200°F for 25 minutes to kill any insect eggs or larvae.

2. Using the pruning shears, cut the pinecone crosswise approximately 2½ inches from the bottom. The lower section will be the nest. Save the top part for a future project.

3. Turn the cone upside down and clip off any petals on what is now the bottom that prevent the cone from sitting flat.

4. Spray the cone with clear acrylic.

5. Halfway down one side of the cone, punch or drill a hole through the middle of a petal. Drill a similar hole on the other side of the cone, directly opposite the first.

6. To make the handle, apply hot glue to the wire, covering a few inches at a time, and wrap the glued area with the Spanish moss. Leave 1 inch of wire bare at each end.

7. Insert the ends of the wire handle through the holes, bend back the wire ends, and twist to secure. Turn the handle at a right angle to the pinecone to create a basket effect.

8. Fill the crevices between the petals with Spanish moss, using the point of the scissors to push the moss into place.

9. Hot-glue a small piece of Spanish moss to the inside of the nest and hot-glue the artificial bird to the moss inside the nest.

Gift Cards

When they're trimmed with delicate greenery and dried flowers, gift cards are almost as welcome as the presents they accompany.

Materials

For the top card:
2 sprigs of white pine, 2 inches long
3 sprigs of caspia, 1 inch long
2 sprigs of white annual statice
Pen
Blank gift card
Hot-glue gun and glue sticks

For the card at left:
2 sprigs of sweet Annie, 2 inches long

1 sprig of caspia, 1 inch long
2 cinnamon sticks, one 2½ inches long
    and one 1 inch long
Pen
Blank gift card
Hot-glue gun and glue sticks

For the card at right:
2 sprigs of white pine, 1½ inches long
1 dried red rosebud
Pen
Blank gift card
Hot-glue gun and glue sticks

1. First write the gift recipient's name on the card. Addressing the card after it is decorated may damage delicate materials.

2. Hot-glue the decorative materials one at a time to the top left corner of the card, affixing them in the order given.

Twig Ornament

Almost everyone's backyard boasts a few fallen twigs with interesting-looking fungus attached. If the size and shape are right, bring them inside and give them a chance to dress up another tree.

Materials

- 2 pinecones, small enough to fit inside the mushroom (below)
- 4- to 5-inch twig with mushroom attached
- 3 sprigs of greenery, such as ming fern or pine
- 1½ yards of red velvet ribbon, ¼ inch wide
- Scissors
- Hot-glue gun and glue sticks
- Artificial bird, 2 to 3 inches long from beak to tail

1. Bake the pinecones at 200°F for 25 minutes to kill any insect eggs or larvae.

2. Cut the ribbon into three pieces, one 10 inches long, one 12 inches long, and one 24 inches long. Set aside the remaining 8-inch length for a future project.

3. To make a hanger, fold the 10-inch piece of ribbon in half and hot-glue both ends to the back of the twig, near what will be the top of the ornament. Wrap the 12-inch piece of ribbon around the twig, concealing the hanger ends and helping to hold them in place. Hot-glue the ends of the wrapped ribbon to the back of the ornament.

4. Tie the 24-inch length of ribbon into a bow and hot-glue it to the front of the twig.

5. Using the photo as a guide, hot-glue the bird to the top edge of the mushroom and glue the pinecones inside the mushroom.

6. Tuck the greenery around the bird and hot-glue the ends in place.

Trim your tree with pinecone bird nests
(see page 150), a twig ornament (see page 153),
a pine needle basket (see page 156),
a sweet gum candy cane (see page 159),
a hot-air balloon (see page 190), and
a cinnamon stick ornament (see page 207).

Pine Needle Basket

Wherever pine trees grow, people have coiled pine needles to make containers. You can use this centuries-old technique to make a few baskets for your Christmas tree.

Materials

For one basket ornament:

1 English walnut

15 longleaf pine needle clusters, caps on

Spanish moss

Coping saw

Paring knife

Electric drill with $\frac{1}{16}$-inch bit

Large pot or heat-proof bowl

Boiling water

Brown quilting thread

Heavy-duty scissors

Needle

Hot-glue gun with glue sticks

Clothespins

Acrylic spray

Decorative materials of your choice
   (see below)

12 inches of red velvet ribbon, $\frac{1}{4}$ inch wide

6 inches of string

Decorative Materials

For the bear ornament:

Flocked teddy bear, 1 inch high, with acorn
   shell hot-glued to head

4 hemlock cones

4 tiny dried red flowers

4 pieces of greenery, 1 inch long

For the mouse ornament:

2 wooden craft mice, $\frac{1}{2}$ inch long

Birdseed

2 tiny dried red flowers

For the bird ornament:

1 red artificial bird, $1\frac{1}{2}$ inches long from beak
   to tail

2 hemlock cones

Sprig of dried white flowers

1. Using the coping saw, cut the English walnut in half lengthwise, along the natural indentation in the nut. Clean out the nut meat and membranes with a paring knife. Select one nutshell half for this project and save the other for a future project.

2. Using the electric drill and the 1/16-inch bit, drill a row of holes around the rim of the nutshell, spacing them about 1/4 inch apart.

3. Put the pine needles into the pot and pour boiling water over them to cover. Allow the needles to soak for approximately 1 hour. Pour off the water and wrap the needles in a towel to keep them soft and pliable.

4. With the quilting thread, tie three pine needle clusters together just below their caps. Cut off the caps with the scissors as closely as possible to the tied thread.

5. Thread the needle with the quilting thread. Place the tied bundle of pine needles along the rim of the walnut. Working from the inside to the outside, bring the needle through one of the drilled holes, back over the pine needle coil, and through the adjacent hole. Continue from hole to

Figure 1

Figure 2

hole around the nut until you have whipstitched the coil to the rim of the nut (see Figure 1). When you return to your starting point, knot the thread and hide the knot by tucking it into the coil.

6. As you begin the second coiled row, you must add additional needles to the bundle to make a continual coil. Cut the cap off a pine needle cluster and insert the needles into the middle of the coil. Add a new pine needle cluster every few stitches to keep the coil going.

7. Using the same technique you just used to sew the first coil to the walnut, sew the second coil to the first, using the stitches on the first row as guides. As the pine needle bundle begins to circle the nut for the second time and thus form the second row, continue to work from inside to outside. Place the needle just to the right of the stitch immediately below. Take the needle through the top portion of the first coil and bring it back over the top of the second coil. Now move to the next stitch to the right. Again, insert the needle immediately to the right of that stitch, and repeat the process (see Figure 2). Continue adding needles and whipstitching coils to each other until you have three coils.

8. As you come to the end of your third coil, stop adding needles so that the bundle will taper. If necessary, cut out some needles in the center of the coil.

9. Bring the needle around the last coil once more and knot the thread on the inside of the basket. Clip off the thread ends.

10. Set the basket aside to dry.

11. To make the handle, tie three pine needle clusters together with quilting thread just below their caps. Separate the needles into three equal sections and braid them all the way to the other end. Tie off the other end with quilting thread. Trim the caps off one end and stray pine needle ends off the other. Hot-glue the handle to the basket, positioning the ends inside the basket and using clothespins to hold the ends in place until the glue sets.

12. Spray the basket with clear acrylic and allow it to dry.

13. Fill the basket with Spanish moss and hot-glue the decorative materials to the moss. Make a four-loop bow with the ribbon and tie it to the center of the handle with the string. Knot the ends of the string to form a hanger. (See "Making Bows" on page 30.)

Sweet Gum Candy Canes

Seedpods from a sweet gum tree add a prickly new texture to traditional red-striped candy canes.

Materials

12 sweet gum seedpods

4 pinecones, ½ inch long (optional)

8 pieces of hemlock, 2 inches long (optional)

6 small craft berries (optional)

Floral fixative spray

Hot-glue gun and glue sticks

10-inch piece of metallic string

1 yard of red velvet ribbon, ¼ inch wide

½ yard of red velvet ribbon, ¼ inch wide (optional)

1. Spray the seedpods with floral fixative and allow them to dry.

2. Hot-glue the seedpods together in a candy cane shape. For maximum holding power, hot-glue two seedpods together and hold them in place for a few seconds until the glue is dry. Then glue another seedpod to the cane and allow it to dry, continuing in this fashion until the cane is complete.

3. To make a hanger, form the metallic string into a loop and tie the ends in a knot. Hot-glue the knot to the back of the candy cane, just where it starts to curve.

4. Hot-glue the 1-yard piece of ribbon to the back of the candy cane at the tip of the curved end. Wrap the ribbon around the cane in a spiral fashion so that the ribbon falls between the seedpods on the side you have designated as the front. Hot-glue the other end of the ribbon to the bottom of the cane on the back.

5. If desired, form a bow with the ½-yard piece of ribbon and hot-glue it to the cane. Hot-glue the hemlock pieces, pinecones, and berries to the center of the bow.

Painted Eggs

It doesn't take a trained eye or a hand experienced with a paintbrush to produce these delightful painted ornaments. The simple Christmas motifs we mastered as children have a charm all their own, especially when applied to pristine white eggs.

Materials

For one egg:

White large or extra-large egg

Fork or small, sharp nail

Bowl

Acrylic paints

Small paintbrush

Clear acrylic spray

9-inch piece of medium-gauge gold wire

2 beads, 3 millimeters in circumference

2 beads, 8 millimeters in circumference

2 decorative sequins, ½ inch in diameter

Wire cutters or heavy-duty scissors

1. Wash the egg and pat it dry.

2. With a fork tine or a small, sharp nail, make a small hole in the narrow end of the egg (this will be the top). Make a slightly larger hole in the wide end (this will be the bottom).

3. Shake the egg yolk and white down to the bottom. Working over a bowl, blow on the top hole, forcing the white and yolk out of the bottom. Rinse the inside of the shell with water and blow it out. Set the shell aside and allow it to dry.

4. With the acrylic paints, paint a design on the eggshell in the colors of your choice using one of the patterns in Figure 5 on page 163 as a guide. When the paint is completely dry, spray it with the clear acrylic.

5. To make a hanger, bring the ends of the gold wire together and twist them together to form a ¼-inch-diameter loop (see Figure 1).

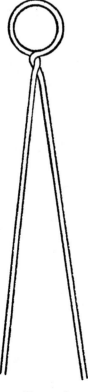

Figure 1

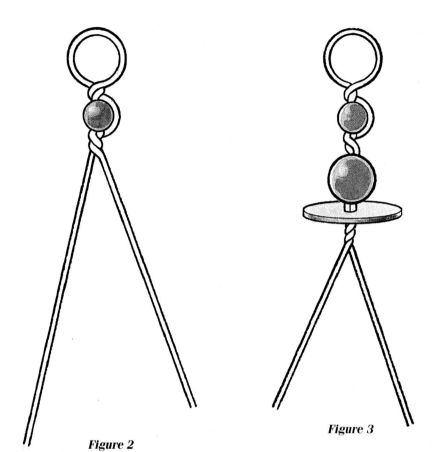

Figure 2

Figure 3

Figure 4

6. Insert one wire end through a 3-millimeter bead, pushing the bead up against the loop. Bring the two wires together below the bead and twist them several times (see Figure 2).

7. Insert both wires through an 8-millimeter bead, then through a sequin, and twist the wires together (see Figure 3).

8. Insert both wires through the top hole in the egg, working them through the eggshell and out the bottom hole.

9. At the bottom of the egg, insert both wires through a sequin, then through an 8-millimeter bead, and then through a 3-millimeter bead.

10. Gently separate the wires as far as they will go, forcing the bottom beads tight against the egg. Bring the wire ends back up over the 3-millimeter bead, with one wire on each side (see Figure 4). Twist the wires around the juncture of the small and large beads. Clip off the wire ends with the wire cutters, and tuck any remaining ends between the beads.

Figure 5

Cornhusk Tree Topper

This lovely cornhusk doll radiates with the beauty of handcrafted Christmas items. She is fairly simple to make, and after the holidays, the holiday trimmings can be replaced with faux pearls so she can be enjoyed year 'round.

Materials

- 30 to 40 clean, white cornhusks
- Cornsilks
- 12 stems of dried caspia, 4 inches long
- 4 stems of cedar (or other evergreen), 4 inches long
- 2 dried feverfew blooms
- 5 small love-in-a-mist blooms
- Large towel, folded in half several times
- Foam ball, 1-inch diameter
- Dental floss
- Scissors
- White craft glue
- Hair spray
- 24-ounce paper cup
- Miniature basket
- Scrap of floral foam
- Tea bag
- Rectangle of gauze, 4 × 20 inches
- 5 lengths of strung cranberries or 8 mm beading, one 14 inches long and four 4 inches long
- 14-inch piece of gold cord
- Gold pipe cleaner (optional)

1. Place the towel on a flat surface to form a protected work area.

2. Soak the cornhusks in warm water for a few minutes until they are soft and pliable.

3. Place the foam ball in the center of a wide cornhusk. Fold the husk over and roll it tightly around the ball so no foam shows, then twist the husk at the top and bottom.

4. Bring one twisted end down to the other and bind them together tightly with floss. (Your work will look like a balloon with a long tail.) This will be the head.

5. Arrange two cornhusks end to end with their narrow ends overlapping about 2 inches and roll them into a cigar shape. Fold each end back toward the center point and secure them with a short length of dental floss. You will now have an arm piece about 6 inches long.

6. To form the hands, tie a short length of dental floss about 1/4 inch in from each folded end of the piece you made in Step 5, and trim off any excess floss.

7. Pull the "tail" section of head apart and insert the center of the arm piece up against the head, just at the neck. Bring the tails back down and wrap several folded pieces of cornhusks around the neck and arm piece like a shawl to form a padded upper body.

8. Create the doll's skirt by arranging cornhusks (narrow ends facing up) around the waist. Continue adding cornhusks until you're happy with the fullness of the skirt, and then secure them in the waist area with several wraps of dental floss.

9. Trim the skirt's hemline until the doll stands balanced. If desired, several of the outer cornhusks can be trimmed a few inches shorter or scalloped to create a layered effect in the skirt.

10. Drip some glue over the doll's head, then dampen the cornsilks with water and work them around the head to form hair. Finish with a light spritz of hair spray.

11. To form the bonnet, fold a cornhusk in half lengthwise and wrap it around the head with the folded edge facing the front. Shape the back of the bonnet and tie it in place around the head with a short length of dental floss.

12. Finish the bonnet by wrapping an 8 × 2-inch strip of cornhusk around the front of the bonnet and securing it in the top front with two knots. Trim off any excess cornhusk around the bonnet or the tie.

13. Wrap and tie a narrow band of cornhusks around the waist to cover the floss, and cut any cornhusk tips that protrude above the waistband.

14. Bend and shape the arms, dampening them with a little water if necessary. Open the skirt and place the doll on a paper cup to dry.

15. Cut a small piece of floral foam to fit inside the basket and wedge it in place. When the doll has dried, glue the center of the basket handle to one of the doll's hands. Insert the dried flowers into the foam with the caspia stems first, then the evergreens, then the feverfew blooms, and the delicate love-in-a-mist blooms last.

16. Prepare a cup of tea with the tea bag, then add 2 cups of water to the tea to make a weak dye bath.

17. Soak the gauze in the tea dye for 1 hour. While it's still damp, fold the gauze around the doll's neck to form a shawl, tucking it under and around the arms and allowing it to drape down the skirt.

18. Add some holiday cheer to the basket by placing the 4-inch lengths of strung cranberries or beading among the blooms, then finish by tying a cranberry and gold cord necklace around the neck. If desired, the doll can be converted into an angel by folding the gold pipe cleaner in a halo shape and gluing it to the back of the head.

Floral Bouquet Tree Topper

A showy tree topper can become the focal point of a Christmas tree. This bouquet of flowers and fruit is set off with scarlet streamers to cascade down the tree.

Materials

  7 dried red roses, one 6 inches long and six 1½ inches long

  48 heads of santolina, stems 6 inches long

  6 sprigs of baby's-breath, 6 inches long

  12 stems of salvia, 7 inches long

  6 cinnamon sticks, 3 inches long

  6 dried orange slices (See "Drying Fruit" on page 28.)

  7 stems of pearly everlasting, 7 inches long

  6 white globe amaranth blooms

  Floral tape

  4 rubber bands

  Scissors

  Purchased nosegay holder with border of green paper leaves

  Hot-glue gun and glue sticks

  12 yards of red velvet cord, cut into four 3-yard pieces

  Medium-gauge floral wire

1. Wrap floral tape around the stem of the 6-inch-long rose to strengthen it. (See "Floral Tape" on page 17.)

2. Divide the santolina into four bunches and wrap the stems of each bunch with a rubber band. Position the bunches around the rose and tape all the floral stems together.

3. Insert sprigs of baby's-breath between the santolina.

4. Arrange the salvia around the outside of the bouquet and tape to the bunched santolina.

5. Tape the cinnamon sticks and then the pearly everlasting evenly around the outside of the bouquet.

6. Slip the orange slices vertically into the bouquet just inside the row of pearly everlasting.

7. Tape all stems tightly and trim the bottoms evenly to about 6 inches.

8. Insert the bouquet in the nosegay holder and tape again, beginning at the base of the cuff.

9. Hot-glue the six roses with 1½-inch stems between the cinnamon sticks. Then hot-glue the six globe amaranth blooms randomly over the surface of the bouquet, filling in any empty spaces.

10. With one length of red velvet cord, make a six-loop bow with one 20-inch streamer and one 42-inch streamer. Make three additional bows in the same fashion with the remaining cord.

11. Space the four bows evenly around the base of the nosegay so that the loops are continuous, and tape them to the nosegay under the cuff. For this final taping, make sure the bottom of the nosegay is neat and tidy.

12. Wire the nosegay to the top of the tree, arranging the streamers so that they hang down on all sides of the tree.

Floral Horns

*Trumpet your joy in the Christmas season with miniature
brass horns decorated with herbs and flowers.*

Materials

For one ornament:

2 mountain mint leaves (ornament on left)
or 6 bay leaves on their stems
(ornament on right)

2 lavender flowers

2 heads of cockscomb, 2 inches in diameter

2 pink rosebuds, 1 inch long

2 santolina blooms

2-inch sprig of sweet Annie

1 strawflower

4 sprigs of baby's-breath, 2 inches long

Hot-glue gun and glue sticks

5- to 6-inch brass horn with red cord
and tassel

Floral fixative spray

1. Hot-glue the mountain mint or bay
leaves to the horn, with their stems overlapping.

2. Hot-glue the remaining flowers and
foliage to the ornament in the order given,
using the photo as a guide or arranging
them in a pattern of your own choosing.

3. Spray the finished arrangement with
floral fixative.

Blown Glass Ornaments

Plain glass balls that sparkle in the Christmas lights are fine ornaments for the tree. Decorated with flowers, foliage, and bows, they become unique and personal ornaments.

Materials

For the top ornament:

4 to 6 sprigs of spruce or pine

4 to 6 sprigs of German statice, 2 inches long

1 cluster of pearly everlasting, 2 inches wide

Hot-glue gun and glue sticks

Glass Christmas ball

1 yard of red-and-green-striped wired ribbon, 1 inch wide

For the bottom ornament:

6 to 10 sprigs of cedar

6 to 8 sprigs of German statice, 2 inches long

1 cluster of pearly everlasting, 2 inches wide

1 red cockscomb head, 2 inches wide

Hot-glue gun and glue sticks

Glass Christmas ball

1 yard of red grosgrain ribbon, ½ inch wide

1. Hot-glue the sprigs of greenery around the top of the ornament.

2. Next, hot-glue the German statice on top of the greenery.

3. Make a bow from the ribbon and hot-glue it to the top of the ornament. (See "Making Bows" on page 30.)

4. Hot-glue the pearly everlasting and the cockscomb, if used, on top of the other flowers or inside the loops of the bow.

Sweet Gum Mini Wreath

Seedpods from the sweet gum tree make an attractive base for a mini wreath. Plant materials adhere to their prickly surfaces extremely well.

Materials

7 sweet gum seedpods

1 stem of ming fern or hemlock, 10 inches long, cut into pieces ½ inch long

1 stem of pink larkspur, cut into small pieces

1 to 2 stems of white ti tree, cut into small pieces

Hot-glue gun and glue sticks

15 inches of pink satin ribbon, 1¼ inch wide, cut into one 9-inch piece and one 6-inch piece

1. To make the wreath base, hot-glue the sweet gum pods against each other in a circle, as shown in the photo (above left).

2. Make a loop with the 9-inch piece of ribbon and hot-glue the ends to the back of the base.

3. Hot-glue the foliage and flowers to the wreath base—first the ming fern or hemlock, then the larkspur, and finally the ti tree.

4. Make a two-loop bow with the 6-inch piece of ribbon and hot-glue it to the front of the ornament. Glue a piece of larkspur to the center of the bow, if desired.

Fabulous Fruit Ornaments

A favorite food of just about everyone, fruit is famous for its jewel-tone colors as well as for its fragrance and flavor. Preserved whole or in slices, it adds color and interest to the Christmas tree.

Decorated Pomegranate

Materials

 1 dried pomegranate

 4 bay leaves

 3 sprigs of baby's-breath, 2 inches long

 2 dried pink roses

 3 sprigs of larkspur, 2 inches long

 2 globe amaranths

 15 inches of raffia

 Hot-glue gun and glue sticks

 Floral fixative spray

1. Tie a knot in the center of the raffia and hot-glue the knot to the flat end of the pome-granate. Knot the raffia "tails" so that they form a hanger loop for the ornament.

2. Hot-glue three bay leaves around the knot in a triangular arrangement, with the tips of the leaves pointing outward.

3. Hot-glue the flowers around the top of the ornament, distributing them evenly and covering the pomegranate end.

4. Check to see that the ornament is evenly balanced. If there are any remaining holes in the design, hot-glue the remaining bay leaf in the open area, slipping it under the flowers.

5. Spray the flower arrangement with the floral fixative.

Orange and Bay Leaf Ornament

Materials

 1 dried orange slice (See "Drying Fruit" on page 28.)

 2 bay leaves

 2 cinnamon sticks, 3 inches long

 1 star anise

 2 whole allspice

 31 inches of raffia, cut into one 16-inch piece and one 15-inch piece

 Needle

 Hot-glue gun and glue sticks

1. Thread the needle with the 16-inch piece of raffia and poke it through the orange slice close to the peel, pulling until the ends of the raffia are even. Tie the raffia in a knot right next to the orange peel, leaving long raffia "tails."

2. Hot-glue the bay leaves to the orange slice, positioning them diagonally and placing one over the hole created by the raffia.

3. Hot-glue the cinnamon sticks on top of the bay leaves and glue the star anise to the center of the cinnamon sticks.

4. Hot-glue the allspice to the bay leaves on either side of the star anise.

5. Make a six-loop bow with the 15-inch piece of raffia. (See "Making Bows" on page 30.) Tie the long raffia tails around the bow.

Black Walnut Garland

Concealed within their rough exteriors, walnuts have interesting shapes and patterns. Walnut slices can be threaded with ribbon for a fine-looking natural garland.

Materials

25 to 30 black walnuts

Coping saw

Red fabric dye or spray paint

Clear acrylic spray

10 feet of white cord with wire center, ⅛-inch-diameter, cut into two 5-foot pieces

½-inch-wide white masking tape

Tape measure

1. Using the coping saw, cut the walnuts into slices about ¼ inch thick (see Figure 1), cutting parallel to the natural seam of the nut. Clean out any meat or unsightly pieces of

Figure 1

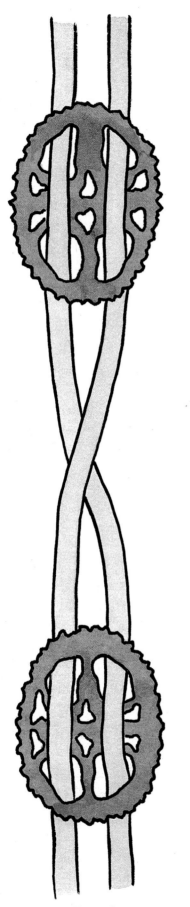

membrane. Select eight to ten slices approximately the same size for this project.

2. Dye the nut slices with the red fabric dye, following the package instructions for dyeing wood. Fabric dye produces a relatively subdued color. Fabric dye was used on the garland pictured, with every fourth slice left its natural color. If a brighter finish is desired, spray the nut slices with red spray paint. In either case, allow the slices to dry.

3. Spray all the walnut slices with acrylic spray.

4. Wrap the ends of the cord with masking tape to facilitate threading and prevent fraying.

5. Thread one piece of cord through the holes of a nut slice, entering from the back and exiting the front. Thread the second piece of cord through the same nut slice in a similar fashion (see Figure 2). The nut slice should be about 4 inches from the end of both cords.

6. Measure about 2 inches from the first nut slice and twist the cords. Secure the twist with a piece of masking tape.

7. Measure another 2 inches from the twist and thread the second nut slice onto the cords in the same fashion. Continue until the garland is complete, making sure that every fourth slice is undyed (if that is the pattern you've chosen) and leaving 4 inches of cord at the end.

8. Drape the garland on the Christmas tree and twist each wired cord end to a branch.

Figure 2

Pine Needle Birdcage

*This woven-pine birdcage makes
a distinctive tree topper.*

Materials

80 longleaf pine needle clusters, caps on

4-inch-diameter piece of sphagnum moss

6 sprigs of German statice, 2 inches long

2 sprigs of baby's-breath, 1½ inches in diameter

2 dried blue starflowers

Large pot or heat-proof bowl

Boiling water

Brown quilting thread

3 pieces of medium-gauge floral wire,
    25 inches long

Heavy-duty scissors

Darning needle

Paintbrush

Shellac

Hot-glue gun and glue sticks

Artificial red bird, 1 inch long from beak
    to tail

1 yard of white satin ribbon, ³⁄₁₆ inch wide,
    cut into two 18-inch-long pieces

1. Put the pine needle clusters into the pot or bowl and pour enough boiling water over them to cover. Allow the needles to soak for approximately 1 hour.

2. Make a bundle of six pine needle clusters by tying them together with the quilting thread just below their caps. Divide the bundle into three equal groups.

3. Insert one 25-inch piece of wire up the middle of the center group so that the top of the wire protrudes about 1 inch above the top of the caps.

4. Begin by braiding four times: that is, bring the right-hand group of needles over the center group, then the left-hand group over the center group, then the right over the center, then the left over the center.

5. Insert another pine needle cluster into the braid, positioning it over the right-hand group and under the center one, with its cap pointing to the right and protruding from the braid about ¼ inch (see Figure 1 on page 184).

6. Continue braiding, inserting an extra pine needle cluster after every four braids until you have added 20 needle clusters and you have a braid about 19 inches long.

7. Secure the finished braid by wrapping the wire around it several times near the end, leaving about 1 inch of unbraided needles. Trim off the top and bottom wire ends with scissors. Snip off any pine needles sticking out along the braid and trim the end of the braid so that the loose needles are even.

8. Make two more pine needle braids about 19 inches long, using the instructions in steps 2 through 7.

9. Bend one of the braids into a teardrop shape and sew it together just below the caps on one end and the loose needles on the other end, using the darning needle and quilting thread. Repeat the process for the other two braids.

10. Insert one braided teardrop inside another one with the sides at right angles and sew the two together at top and bottom (see Figure 1). Insert the third braided teardrop inside the second, adjusting its sides so that they are equidistant from the sides of the adjoining braids. Sew through all three braids at top and bottom. At the bottom of the birdcage, the three braids will be stacked on top of each other.

11. Select a pine needle cluster and divide the needles into three roughly equal groups. Braid to the end of the needles and tie off the ends with quilting thread. Form the braided needle cluster into a loop for the bird's perch and tie the two ends together below the cap. Cut off the cap.

12. Thread the darning needle with a length of quilting thread and use it to form a slipknot around the top of the perch. Place the perch inside the birdcage and bring the needle up through the top of the birdcage. Leaving the perch loose enough to swing easily, wrap the thread around the tied top of the cage and knot the thread (see Figure 2).

13. Using the paintbrush, apply a heavy coat of shellac to the birdcage. Push down on the top of the cage to create a rounded shape. While the cage is drying, check its shape from time to time, pushing down on the top if necessary.

14. Hot-glue the sphagnum moss to the bottom of the birdcage and hot-glue the bird to its perch.

15. Make two bows with the pieces of white satin ribbon and hot-glue them opposite each other on the top of the birdcage. Hot-glue the sprigs of German statice in the spaces between the bows and hot-glue the sprigs of baby's-breath into the bows themselves. Lay the two dried blue starflowers on the bottom of the cage.

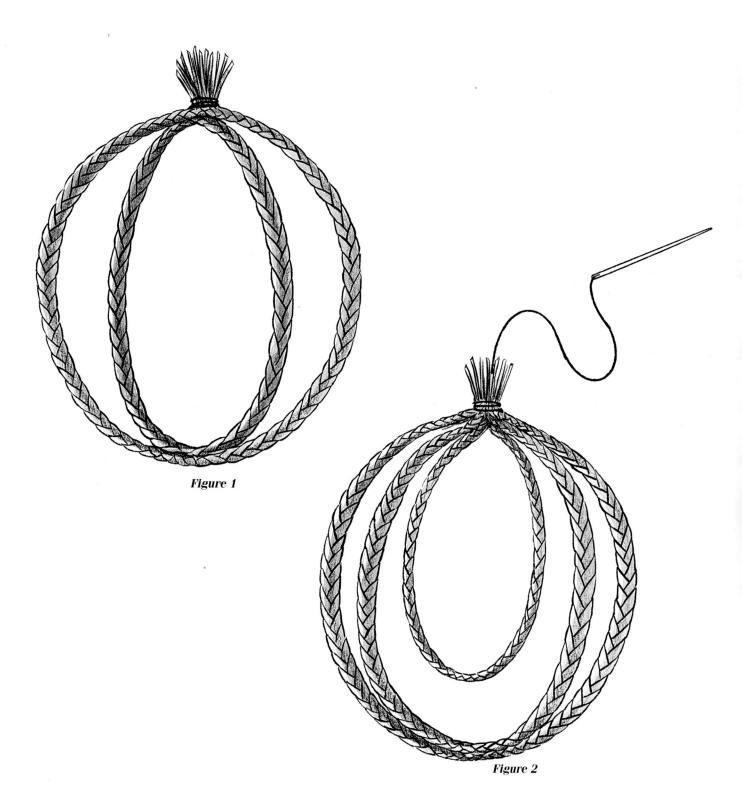

Figure 1

Figure 2

These attractive tree trimmers are quick and easy to make. Try crafting a pine needle basket (see page 156), a painted egg (see page 160), a floral horn (see page 169), a braided pine ornament (see page 183), an okra ornament (see page 185), a found ornament (see page 186), a gourd ornament (see page 191), and a cinnamon stick ornament (see page 207).

Braided Pine Ornaments

Wreaths and bells are well-loved Christmas motifs, and fragrant, supple pine needles can be braided and then coaxed into both of these shapes.

Materials

For one bell or one wreath:

18 longleaf pine needle clusters, caps on

3 hemlock cones, or other small cones

2 pieces of preserved green fern, 2 inches long

Cluster of tiny dried white flowers, ½ inch in diameter and 1 inch long

Large pot or heat-proof bowl

Boiling water

Quilting thread, or other strong thread

Wire cutters or heavy-duty scissors

Medium-gauge floral wire

Bell-shaped form

6 to 8 rubber bands (for the bell)

Acrylic spray

14 inches of red velvet ribbon, ³⁄₁₆ inch wide

Hot-glue gun and glue sticks

10-inch piece of gold or silver string

1. Put the pine needles into the pot and pour boiling water over them to cover. Allow the needles to soak for approximately 1 hour.

2. Bake the cones at 200°F for 25 minutes to kill any insect eggs or larvae.

3. Make a bundle of six needle clusters by tying them together with the thread just below their caps. Divide the bundle evenly into three groups.

4. Using the wire cutters or scissors, cut a piece of wire 4 inches longer than the pine needles. Insert the wire into the middle of the center bundle, with the top of the wire flush with the top of the caps and the extra 4 inches of wire protruding from the bottom of the bundle.

5. Begin by braiding four times: that is, bring the right-hand group of needles over the center group, then the left-hand group over the center group, then the right over the center, then the left over the center.

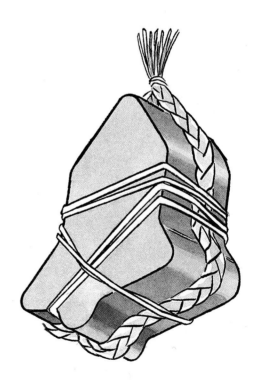

6. Insert another pine needle cluster into the braid, positioning it over the right-hand group and under the center one, with its cap pointing to the right and protruding from the braid about ¼ inch (see Figure 1).

7. Continue braiding, inserting an extra pine needle cluster after every four braids, until all 12 needle clusters have been added.

8. Secure the finished braid by wrapping the wire several times around the end. Trim off the wire ends with the wire cutters or scissors. Snip off any pine needles sticking out along the braid and cut the end of the braid at a slant.

9. *To make a wreath:* Bend the braid into a circle, with the ends overlapping by about 2 inches. Wire the overlapped braid ends together in two places. Allow the wreath to dry overnight.

To make a bell: Wrap the braid tightly around a rigid, bell-shaped form—a cookie cutter, for example, or a piece of wood cut into a bell shape. Wire the ends of the braid together tightly and stretch several rubber bands over the braid and the form, binding the braid in several directions (see Figure 2). If the form is thick enough, you can shape more than one ornament at a time. Allow the bell to dry overnight, then remove it from the form.

10. Spray the ornament with clear acrylic.

11. Take the red velvet ribbon and make a six-loop bow with 3-inch streamers (see "Making Bows" on page 30). Hot-glue it to the top of the ornament.

12. Hot-glue the fern and flowers to the center of the bow. Hot-glue the cones on top of the stems.

13. Tie the gold or silver string in a loop and trim the ends close to the knot. Hot-glue the knot to the back of the ornament.

Figure 1

Figure 2

Okra Ornament

Native to Africa, okra came to the United States with the slave trade. When not being fried as a side dish or simmered in stews, it can be dried and painted as an unusual tree ornament.

Materials

For one ornament:

Okra pod

Acrylic paints

Paintbrush

Black permanent marker
   with very fine tip

Clear varnish spray

Colored string

1. Place the okra pod in a warm, moisture-free place to dry for about two months.

2. Paint a Santa face on the pod, making most of the elongated shape a long, white beard. When the paint is completely dry, sketch in the eyes with the black permanent marker.

3. Spray the ornament with clear varnish.

4. Tie a loop of colored string to the stem to form a hanger.

Found Ornaments

Anything the right size, shape, and weight can be painted with acrylic paints for a light-hearted tree ornament. Here are some made from small pieces of driftwood and fallen pods from the Kentucky coffee tree—so named because early pioneers made a bitter drink from its seeds.

Materials

Small pieces of driftwood or other found materials

Pods from the Kentucky coffee tree or other large pods

Awl or sharp nail

Acrylic paints

Paintbrushes

Clear varnish spray

Colored string

1. Gather the driftwood and pods. Brush off any sand or dirt, and allow the materials to dry for several days.

2. Using the awl or nail, punch a hole close to what will be the top of each ornament.

3. Paint each ornament with acrylic paints in the colors of your choice, using the patterns in Figure 1 as a guide. Allow the paint to dry thoroughly. When dry, spray with clear varnish.

4. To make hangers, thread a piece of colored string through the hole in each ornament, and tie the ends in a knot.

Figure 1

Victorian Tree Ornaments

Popular in the nineteenth century, tussie mussies and pomanders have survived to grace many a modern Christmas tree.

Tussie Mussie Ornament

Materials

- 4 mountain mint leaves
- 1 hemlock cone with petals open
- 6 star anise
- 6 rose hips
- 2 sprigs of baby's-breath, 2 inches in diameter
- 6 lunaria seedpods
- Hot-glue gun and glue sticks
- 3-inch-diameter paper doily cuff for nosegay
- Fine-gauge floral wire
- Green floral tape
- Scissors
- 1 yard of cream ribbon with gold border, ⅛ inch wide, cut into one 26-inch piece and one 10-inch piece

1. Hot-glue the mountain mint leaves around the inside of the cuff, spacing them evenly.

2. Wire the hemlock cone, the star anise, and the rose hips. (See "Floral Wire" on page 17.)

3. Make a nosegay with the cone at the center. Wrap the floral tape around the cone's wire, beginning at the top and spiraling down the wire.

4. Surround the cone with the six star anise and wrap all the stems together with the floral tape.

5. Place the rose hips around the bundle and wrap all the stems together with the floral tape.

6. Hot-glue the baby's-breath to the top of the nosegay between the cone and the star anise.

7. Peel off the outer covering from the lunaria seedpods and remove the seeds. Hot-glue the lunaria membranes between the star anise, bending the stars apart if necessary.

8. Insert the nosegay into the cuff and tape around all the stems again, starting at the base of the cuff.

9. To make a hanger, form the 10-inch length of ribbon into a loop and hot-glue it to an inside edge of the paper cuff.

10. Make a six-loop bow from the 26-inch length of ribbon and wire it together around the center. (See "Making Bows" on page 30.) Clip the wire ends and hot-glue the bow to the inside edge of the cuff, placing it over the glued end of the hanger.

Pomander Ornament

Materials

1 orange

400 cloves (1½ to 2 cups)

5 dried mountain mint leaves

1 hops flower

1 rosebud

2 sprigs of yellow yarrow, ½ inch in diameter

1 sprig purple annual statice, 1 inch in diameter

2 sprigs of baby's-breath, 1 inch in diameter

Medium nail

Food dryer (optional)

2 feet of cream ribbon with gold border,
⅛ inch wide

Hot-glue gun and glue sticks

Floral fixative spray

1. Use the nail to punch a hole in the skin of the orange. Immediately insert a clove in the hole. Repeat this process until the entire orange is completely covered with cloves.

2. To dry the pomander in a food dryer, place the pomander on a shelf in the food dryer and process it at high setting for three 24-hour days or until it is so light that it seems to offer no resistance when lifted. To oven-dry the pomander, place it in the oven with the door slightly open. Dry the pomander at 175°F until it is dry and light. Times will vary, so check its progress regularly after the first 24 hours.

If you plan to use the pomander for only a single Christmas season, you can hang it on a sturdy tree branch without drying it at all. If you don't intend to dry the pomander, select an underripe orange as the base and discard the ornament at the first sign (or scent) of mold.

3. Wrap the ribbon around the pomander and knot it at the top, leaving 6-inch "tails." To make a hanger, knot the tails together to create a loop.

4. Hot-glue the mountain mint leaves around the hanger, butting their stem ends up against the hanger to help it remain upright.

5. Hot-glue the floral materials on top of the mint leaves, distributing the flowers evenly around the hanger.

6. Spray the ornament with floral fixative.

Hot-Air Balloon

A gaily decorated hot-air balloon lifts the spirits, whether it's a 30-foot behemoth or a 3-inch replica.

Materials

Seasoned pear-shaped gourd
    (See "Using Gourds" on page 29.)

Soap

Water

Steel wool

Pencil

Electric drill with 1/8-inch bit

Coping saw

Teaspoon

Acrylic paints in red and white

Paintbrush

Black permanent marker

8 inches of monofilament fishing line

String

1. Soak the gourd in soapy water for 20 minutes and use the steel wool to scrub off all dirt and mold. Allow to dry completely.

2. Using the pencil, draw a line around the neck of the gourd, to divide the balloon from the basket. Also draw four vertical lines from top to bottom, dividing the gourd into four quadrants (see Figure 1).

3. Drill two holes on each vertical line: one 1 inch below the dividing line and one ¼ inch above it. Turn the gourd upside down and drill a hole in the top center of the balloon portion.

4. With the coping saw, cut the gourd at the dividing line.

5. Remove all pulp and seeds by scraping the inside with the teaspoon, and clean the inside with soapy water and steel wool. Let the gourd dry completely.

6. Paint the balloon with the acrylic paints. Add texture to the basket with the black marker, referring to the photo.

7. To make a hanger, insert both ends of the monofilament into the hole in the top of the balloon and tie the ends in a large double knot on the inside of the balloon.

8. Connect the balloon to the basket by tying loops of string through the connecting holes, using the photo as a guide.

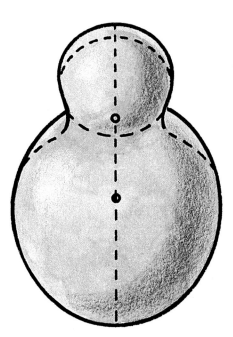

Figure 1

Gourd Ornaments

Although gourds grow in a finite number of overall shapes, they can be painted to resemble a remarkable range of objects, including these cleverly made ornaments—a Santa, a happy baby in a cradle, and an elf.

Santa

Materials

Seasoned bottle gourd, 3 to 5 inches long (See "Using Gourds" on page 29.)

Soap

Water

Steel wool

Awl or sharp nail

Pencil

Black permanent marker with fine point

Acrylic paints in red, gray, brown, black, and beige

1-inch flat paintbrush

Paintbrush with fine tip

Large needle

12-inch piece of red string

1. Soak the gourd in soapy water for 20 minutes and use the steel wool to scrub off all dirt and mold. Allow to dry completely.

2. With the awl or sharp nail, bore two holes opposite each other on the top of the gourd. The holes should be large enough to admit the needle and string.

3. Pencil your design onto the gourd, using Figure 3 on page 195 as a pattern. For lines that will remain visible on the finished Santa—eyes and eyelashes, arms, toys in the sack, for example—go over the pencil lines with the permanent marker.

4. Using the acrylic paints, paint the gourd, beginning with the larger expanses, allowing each color to dry before adding the others.

5. Thread the needle with the red string and pass the needle through both holes in Santa's cap. Remove the needle and tie the ends of the string in a knot to form a loop for hanging.

Baby in a Cradle

Materials

Seasoned bottle gourd, about 2½ inches long, preferably with several vertical indentations (See "Using Gourds" on page 29.)

Scrap piece of another seasoned gourd, in the shape of a cup or cradle, about 2½ inches wide at opening and about 1 inch deep

Soap

Water

Steel wool

Awl or sharp nail

Acrylic paints in white, dark gold, and pink

1-inch flat paintbrush

Black permanent marker with fine tip

Hot-glue gun and glue sticks

3-inch-diameter bunch of natural-colored excelsior

6 inches of medium-gauge floral wire

Large needle

12-inch piece of string

1. Soak the gourd in soapy water for 20 minutes and use the steel wool to scrub off all dirt and mold. Allow to dry completely.

2. With the awl or sharp nail, bore two holes opposite each other on the top of the gourd. The holes should be large enough to admit the needle and string.

3. Paint the gourd white and allow it to dry. Paint on a pink face and gold hair. With the permanent marker, draw the face and darken any interesting indentations in the gourd, to give the impression of fabric folds, using Figure 3 on page 195 as a pattern.

4. Fill the cradle with excelsior and snuggle the baby into the "bedding." Hot-glue the baby to the sides of the cradle.

5. Thread the needle with the string and pass the needle through both holes in the top of the gourd. Remove the needle and tie the ends of the string in a knot to form a loop for hanging.

Elf

Materials

Seasoned bottle gourd, 3½ inches long
(See "Using Gourds" on page 29.)

2 scrap pieces of other seasoned gourds,
each ½ × 1 × ³⁄₁₆ inch

Soap

Water

Steel wool

Electric drill with ¼-inch bit

White craft glue

2 wooden dowels, ¼-inch diameter and 3
inches long

Wood putty

Sharp craft knife

Pencil

Black permanent marker with fine tip

Acrylic paints in green, red, white, yellow,
and brown

1-inch flat paintbrush

Paintbrush with fine tip

5 inches of monofilament fishing line

1. Soak the gourd in soapy water for 20
minutes and use the steel wool to scrub off all
dirt and mold. Allow to dry completely.

2. Using the electric drill and the ¼-inch
bit, drill two holes in the bottom of the gourd,
where the legs will enter.

3. Squeeze a dab of glue on one end of
each dowel and insert the dowels into the
holes in the gourd, pushing the dowels as far
as they will go until the ends rest against the
"shoulders" of the gourd (see Figure 1).
Squeeze a little glue around the dowels where
they enter the gourd and allow to dry. If necessary, fill in any gaps around the legs with
wood putty.

4. Using the sharp craft knife, shape the
two pieces of scrap gourd into "shoes" (see
Figure 2). With the electric drill and ¼-inch
bit, drill a hole through each shoe, toward the
back. Insert the dowels into the holes, positioning the bottom of the dowel flush with
the bottom of the shoe. Glue in place and
allow to dry.

5. Sketch in the rough outlines of the arms
and the gift with the pencil, using Figure 3 as a
pattern. Then go over the pencil marks with the
permanent marker. Paint the elf with the acrylic
paints, using the photo as a guide. Begin with the
larger expanses, allowing each color to dry before
adding the others.

6. Fold the monofilament fishing line into a
loop and glue the ends to the top of the gourd to
act as a hanger.

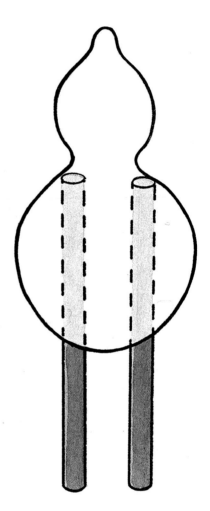

Figure 1

Figure 2

Figure 3

Owl Ornaments

Cut in half, a black walnut seems to observe the world with wise old owl eyes. If you aren't unnerved by a steady gaze, you can make a quick and charming tree ornament from a couple of nuts.

Materials

For one ornament:

1 black walnut half

1 whole black walnut

Sandpaper

Hot-glue gun and glue sticks

8 inches of ribbon, ¼ inch wide

1. Turn the walnut half so that the holes in the cut side resemble owl eyes.

2. Sand the bottom of this "head" and both ends of the whole walnut until somewhat smooth and even.

3. Hot-glue the head to the body.

4. To make a hanger, knot the ends of the ribbon to form a loop and hot-glue the loop to the top of the head.

Pine Needle Broom Ornament

Tidy little brooms are among the easiest pine needle ornaments to make. Decorated with red ribbon and white flowers, they add clean, simple lines to a Christmas tree.

Materials

For one ornament:

78 shortleaf pine needles, caps on

2-inch frond of preserved green fern

Sprig of tiny dried baby's-breath, 1 inch
   long and ½ inch indiameter

2 hemlock cones or other small cones

Large pot or heat-proof bowl

Boiling water

Heavy-duty scissors

Red quilting thread or other strong thread

4 twist-ties

Needle

Clear acrylic spray

14 inches of red velvet ribbon, ³⁄₁₆ inch wide

Hot-glue gun and glue sticks

1. Put the pine needles in the pot and pour boiling water over them to cover. Allow the needles to soak for approximately 1 hour.

2. Make a bundle of 30 pine needles, lining up the ends of the caps evenly.

3. Cut off a 12-inch length of thread, wrap it around the pine bundle just under the caps, and tie a knot. Knot the ends of the thread to form a hanger for the ornament (see Figure 1).

Figure 1

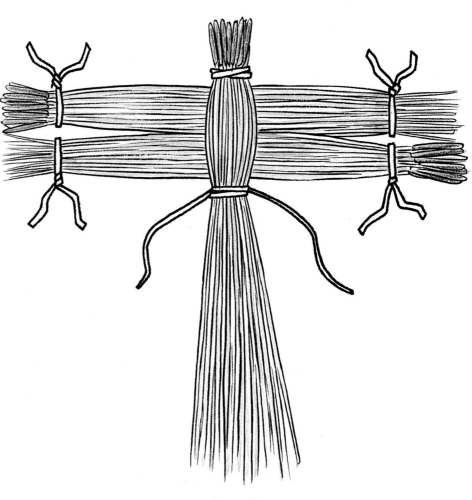

Figure 2

4. Make two bundles with 24 needles each. Secure each bundle temporarily at both ends with the twist-ties.

5. Separate the first bundle in half and insert the two other bundles into the opening, with the caps on one bundle to the right and the caps on the other bundle to the left. Push the two horizonal bundles up as far as possible.

6. Center a 30-inch piece of thread over the vertical bundle, right below the two horizontal bundles, and wrap it around the vertical bundle twice (see Figure 2). Knot the thread, leaving the "tails" free.

7. Thread the needle with the tail at the right of the knot. Bend the lower right-hand horizontal bundle down in an inverted U-shape. Bring the needle around the right bundle and through the middle bundle to secure (see Figure 3). Cross over the middle bundle, encircle the left bundle, and bring the needle through the center bundle to secure.

8. Bend the top horizontal bundle down into an inverted U and sew it to the adjacent bundle in a similar fashion. Bring any loose threads to the front of the ornament and tie them off.

9. Remove the twist-ties, cut the bottom of the broom off evenly, and allow it to dry.

10. Spray the broom with clear acrylic.

11. Make a four-loop bow with 2-inch streamers from the red velvet ribbon and hot-glue it to the front of the broom. (See "Making Bows" on page 30.) Hot-glue the fern, flowers, and cones to the center of the bow.

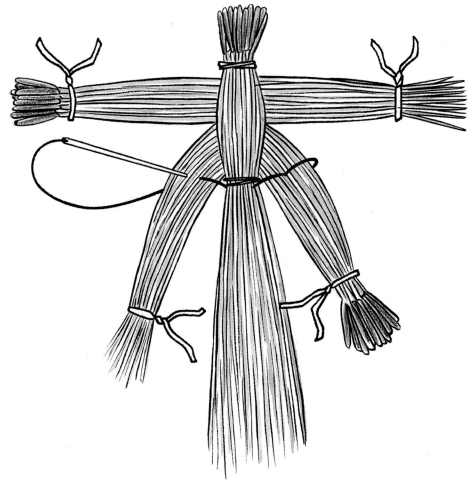

Figure 3

Package Decorations

Nothing dresses up a Christmas tree like handsomely wrapped presents underneath it. These simple-to-make package decorations add a touch of nature to the usual ribbons and bows.

Raffia and Red Flowers

Materials

6 small pinecones

1 decorative pod, such as a poppy pod

4-inch-diameter cluster of dried red starflowers

4 to 6 sprigs of Fraser fir, 6 inches long

10 to 12 fern fronds, 6 inches long

Red gift-wrapping paper

2 yards of raffia, cut into two 1-yard pieces

12 inches of medium-gauge floral wire

Hot-glue gun and glue sticks

1. Bake the pinecones at 200°F for 25 minutes to kill any insect eggs or larvae.

2. Wrap your package with the red wrapping paper and tie it up with raffia. Make a raffia bow and wire it to the crossed pieces of raffia on the front of the package. (See "Making Bows" on page 30.)

3. Hot-glue the pod to the center of the raffia bow and glue the starflowers to the pod. Hot-glue the cones around the bow, distributing them evenly.

4. Hot-glue the greenery—first the Fraser fir, then the ferns—around the bow, passing some of the sprigs and fronds through the loops of the bow.

Cowboy Christmas

Materials

6 sprigs of Fraser fir, 6 inches long

Burlap for wrapping your package

Scissors

2 yards of red ribbon printed with a cowboy motif, 1 inch wide

Hot-glue gun and glue sticks

4 feet of rope, ½-inch diameter

12 inches of medium-gauge floral wire

1. Wrap your package in the burlap, hot-gluing it together where necessary.

2. After cutting off a piece of ribbon long enough for the purpose, hot-glue the ribbon diagonally across the front of the package and down the side, using the photo as a guide.

3. Make a tailored bow with streamers long enough to drape across the front of the box, and hot-glue it to the top corner of the package. (See "Making Bows" on page 30.)

4. Using the photo as a guide, coil the rope into three concentric circles and wire it together. Nestle the coiled rope up against the bow, making sure that the streamers are on top of the rope coil. Hot-glue the top of the coil to the package.

5. Snake one of the bow's streamers through the rope coil, hot-gluing the streamer to the outermost coil.

6. Hot-glue the sprigs of Fraser fir around the bow.

Cinnamon Sticks

Materials

4 cinnamon sticks, 12 inches long

6 sprigs of boxwood, 6 inches long

8 fronds of maidenhair fern, or other feathery fern, 4 inches long

6 sprigs of small white flowers, 3 inches long

Gold foil gift-wrapping paper

Hot-glue gun and glue sticks

2 yards of red ribbon with gold trim, ½-inch-wide

Scissors

Medium-gauge floral wire

Wire cutters

1. Wrap your package in the gold wrapping paper and hot-glue strips of ribbon along the length and width of the package, using the photo as a guide.

2. Form the cinnamon sticks into a bundle and wire them together at the center.

3. Make a bow (see "Making Bows" on page 30) with the remainder of the ribbon and wire it to the center of the cinnamon bundle. Hot-glue the cinnamon bundle to the package in several places.

4. Hot-glue the boxwood, fern, and flowers into the bow.

Spicy Hanging Pomander

Fragrant with all the traditional spices of the season, this scented ornament fairly shouts of Christmas.

Materials

For 12 pomander ornaments:

½ cup of ground cinnamon

3 tablespoons of ground allspice

3 tablespoons of ground cloves

2 tablespoons of ground nutmeg

2 tablespoons of orrisroot granules

1 cup of applesauce

Crochet hook

8 feet of green ribbon, ⅛ inch wide,
    cut into twelve 1-foot pieces

Metal cookie sheet

For decorating one ornament:

4 hemlock cones, or other tiny cones

8 sprigs of German statice, 1 inch long

2 sweet gum seedpods

Petals from 1 red strawflower

22-inch length of metallic green decorative wire

Hot-glue gun and glue sticks

Miniature craft gift package

1. Combine the first five ingredients and mix them well. Stir in the applesauce and mix it thoroughly into the spices. Roll the dough into 12 balls about the size of walnuts.

2. Make a hole through one pomander ball with a crochet hook and thread one piece of ribbon through the hole, using the curved end of the crochet hook to lead the ribbon through the hole. Knot the ends to make a hanger. Repeat the procedure for each pomander.

3. Set the pomanders on a cookie sheet and allow them to dry for seven to ten days, turning them over occasionally.

4. To decorate one pomander, shape the decorative wire into loops that resemble the petals of a daisy and hot-glue them around the pomander.

5. Hot-glue the natural materials to the pomander, using the photo (below, left) as a guide: first the cones, then the German statice, sweet gum pods, and strawflower petals. The photo (below, right) shows the back of an ornament.

6. Finally, hot-glue the miniature gift package to the center of the ornament.

Bird Roosts

No tree is complete without a resident bird. You can offer two house plans, using either a purchased novelty birdhouse or a milkweed pod ornament.

Birdhouse

Materials

- 1½ × 1½-inch clump of garden moss
- 2 mountain mint leaves
- 2 sprigs of sweet Annie, 2 inches long
- 1 lavender flower
- 1½-inch sprig of pearly everlasting
- 2 red globe amaranths
- 1 santolina flower
- Hot-glue gun and glue sticks
- 2 pieces of ⅛-inch-wide red ribbon, 4 inches long
- 1 × 2-inch purchased wooden birdhouse
- 6 inches of elasticized string
- Floral fixative spray

1. Hot-glue one piece of ribbon around the roof of the birdhouse and the other piece around the base.

2. Hot-glue the moss to the roof.

3. To make a hanger, knot the ends of the elasticized string, forming a loop. Hot-glue the knot to the moss, positioning it in the center of the roof.

4. Hot-glue the remaining materials to the moss, covering the roof completely and being careful to leave the hanger free.

5. Spray the arrangement with floral fixative.

Milkweed Pod Ornament

Materials

- 1 milkweed pod
- 1- to 2-inch piece of Spanish moss
- 2 sprigs of caspia or German statice, 2 inches long
- Large-eyed needle
- 48 inches of raffia, cut into one 28-inch piece, one 16-inch piece, and one 4-inch piece
- Hot-glue gun and glue sticks
- 1 artificial cardinal, about 1½ inches from head to tail
- Scissors

1. Open and clean the milkweed pod, removing the membranes and seeds. Save one half for a future project.

2. Thread the needle with the 16-inch piece of raffia and poke the raffia through the remaining milkweed pod half, near the pointed end, about ½ inch down from the tip. Remove the needle and knot the raffia about 2 inches from the ends to form a hanger.

3. Hot-glue the Spanish moss inside the triangular base of the pod.

4. Hot-glue the caspia or German statice into the Spanish moss at the top left and bottom right.

5. Hot-glue the cardinal into the "nest" formed by the moss.

6. Make a 2-inch-diameter bow with the 28-inch piece of raffia, tying it at the center with the 4-inch piece of raffia. (See "Making Bows" on page 30.) Clip the ends with the scissors. Hot-glue the bow to the outside of the pod, below the bird's tail.

Mice in a Nutshell

Actually, a creature is stirring—if not all through the house, then certainly on your Christmas tree.

Materials

For one ornament:

1 English walnut

2-inch-diameter piece of Spanish moss

Coping saw

Sharp craft knife or razor blade

Clear acrylic spray

Hot-glue gun and glue sticks

1 teaspoon of millet birdseed

Wooden craft mouse, about 1 inch long

Tiny dried or silk flowers (optional)

8 inches of metallic thread

1. To make the walnut basket, first find the natural seam of the English walnut. Using the coping saw, make a 1-inch-long cut parallel to the seam line and about $\frac{1}{16}$ inch to the left of it. Make a second parallel cut $\frac{1}{16}$ inch to the right of the seam line.

2. Make two additional cuts perpendicular to the first ones, intersecting them and forming the handle (see Figure 1).

3. Remove the cutout pieces of shell, as well as the meat and membranes. Trim any uneven places with a sharp craft knife or a razor blade and spray the basket with clear acrylic. Allow to dry.

4. When the nut basket is dry, fill it with Spanish moss. Pack the moss down to form a nest. Apply several dabs of hot glue to the surface of the Spanish moss and sprinkle it with birdseed.

5. Glue the wooden mouse into the basket. If desired, glue dried flowers around the mouse.

Cinnamon Stick Ornaments

Sweet, spicy, and warm, the scent of cinnamon is reminiscent of Christmas past. These simple ornaments add that familiar fragrance to your tree.

6. To make a hanger, loop the metallic thread around the handle of the basket and tie the ends together.

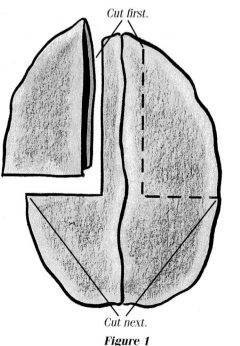

Cut first.

Cut next.

Figure 1

Cinnamon Icicle

Materials

6-inch cinnamon stick

Hemlock cone or other very small cone

4 to 6 boxwood leaves or other green leaves, about 1 inch long

28 inches of red velvet ribbon, ¼ inch wide, cut into two pieces 8 inches long and one piece 12 inches long

Hot-glue gun and glue sticks

1. To make a hanger, fold one 8-inch piece of ribbon in half and hot-glue it about ½ inch from an end of the cinnamon stick, with one end of the ribbon on each side of the stick.

2. Wrap the 12-inch piece of ribbon around the cinnamon stick in a spiral fashion, hot-gluing the ribbon to the stick at both ends.

3. Make a simple bow from the second 8-inch piece of ribbon and hot-glue it to the top of the cinnamon stick.

4. Hot-glue the cone to the center of the bow, then glue the boxwood leaves around it.

Cinnamon-Orange Stick

Materials

6-inch cinnamon stick

2 dried orange slices (See "Drying Fruit" on page 28.)

6 dried green leaves, 1 inch long (See "Working with Flowers and Herbs" on page 26.)

2 dried red starflowers

20 inches of raffia, cut into one 8-inch piece and one 12-inch piece

Hot-glue gun and glue sticks

1. To make a hanger, fold the 8-inch piece of raffia in half and hot-glue it about ½ inch from an end of the cinnamon stick, with one end of the raffia on each side of the stick.

2. Wrap the 12-inch piece of raffia around the top of the cinnamon stick, covering the ends of the hanger and holding them in place. Hot-glue in place.

3. Slide one dried orange slice about three-quarters of the way down the cinnamon stick. Hot-glue the other orange slice flat against the stick, underneath the first slice (see photo).

4. Hot-glue three leaves to the top of the stick in a trefoil pattern and three leaves to the bottom of the horizontal orange slice.

5. Hot-glue one starflower in the center of the trefoil and the other flower to the juncture of the two orange slices (see photo).

Pine Needle Doll Ornament

The nostalgic charm of these old-fashioned dolls echoes a time when hardworking parents took a few moments to make toys for their children out of whatever materials were available—including pine needles.

Materials

For the girl ornament:

33 longleaf pine needle clusters, caps on (6 additional pine needle clusters needed for the boy)

Large pot or heat-proof bowl

Boiling water

Towel

Brown quilting thread

4 twist-ties

Clear acrylic spray

10 inches of red velvet ribbon, $\frac{1}{16}$ inch wide, cut into one 8-inch piece and one 2-inch piece (2 additional 3-inch pieces needed for the boy)

Hot-glue gun and glue sticks

Triangle of red felt, $2\frac{1}{2}$ inches high and 2 inches wide at the base

Pair of artificial holly leaves, 1 inch wide

1. Put the pine needles into the pot and pour boiling water over them to cover. Allow the needles to soak for approximately 1 hour. Pour off the water and wrap the needles in a towel to keep them soft and pliable.

2. To make the body, form 17 pine needle clusters into a bundle, making sure that their caps are even. Tie them together with the thread just under the caps.

3. To make the arms, form eight pine needle clusters into a bundle, again checking that the caps are even, and secure them with one twist-tie $\frac{1}{2}$ inch below the caps and another twist-tie 2 inches from the other end.

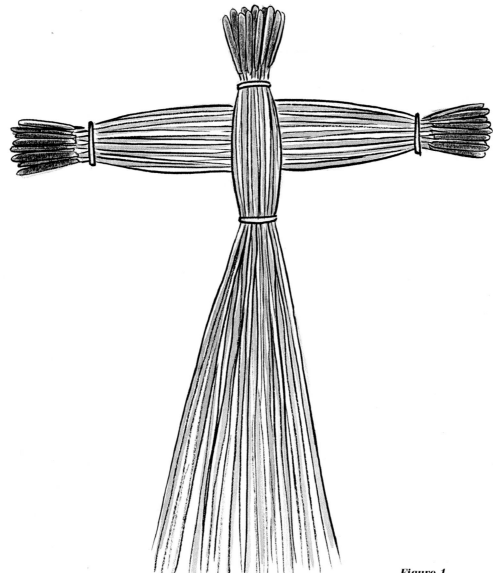

Figure 1

4. Repeat Step 3.

5. Lay the two arm bundles together with the two sets of caps on opposite ends. Using the quilting thread, tie the two bundles together twice at each end, once just below the caps and again ½ inch in from the first set of ties. Remove the twist-ties.

6. Divide the needles in the body section in half and insert the arm bundle, pushing it as high as it will go and flattening it somewhat in the middle. Tie the body tightly just below the arm bundle (see Figure 1).

7. Trim the bottom of the pine needles evenly. *For the boy:* Add three pine needles to the front and three to the back, positioning the bottom of the caps at the tied "waist" of the doll. Tie the needles on with thread, just under the caps (see

Figure 2). Separate the bottom of the body in the middle to form legs, and tie off each leg. Trim the pine needles ½ inch below the leg ties.

8. Spray the ornament with clear acrylic and allow it to dry.

9. To make a hanger, form the 8-inch piece of ribbon into a loop and hot-glue it to the back of the "neck."

10. Decorate the dolls as shown in the photo. *For the girl:* Tie the 2-inch piece of ribbon around the neck in a two-loop bow. Hot-glue the felt skirt into place, as shown in the photo, and hot-glue the holly leaves at the waist. *For the boy:* Hot-glue a 3-inch piece of ribbon down the outside of each leg and tie the 2-inch piece of ribbon around the waist. Hot-glue the holly leaves at the neck.

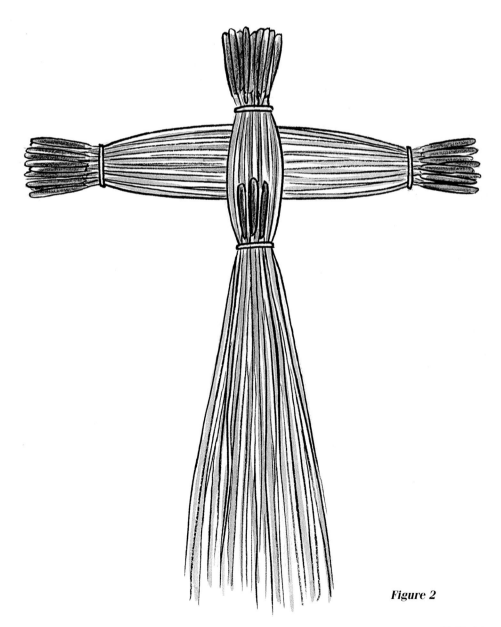

Figure 2

Bay Tree Package

According to ancient legend, bay leaves can ward off witches on errands of mischief. Perhaps bay leaves can also ward off gremlins on premature forays into the stacks of presents under the tree!

Materials

23 bay leaves

8 to 10 pieces of cinnamon stick, one 3 inches long, the remainder ½ inch long

6 star anise

4 to 6 rose hips

7 to 10 whole allspice

17 × 11 × 2-inch gift box

36 × 36 inch sheet of shiny, white gift-wrapping or floral paper

Hot-glue gun and glue sticks

Floral fixative spray

Artificial bird, 2 inches long from beak to tail

1. Wrap the gift box in the white wrapping paper.

2. Beginning at the top, hot-glue the bay leaves to the package in a tree shape, with each row overlapping the previous one. Hot-glue extra bay leaves to the tree as necessary to fill in any spaces.

3. Hot-glue the 3-inch cinnamon stick "trunk" to the bottom of the tree.

4. Hot-glue one star anise at the top of the tree and the remaining five in a zigzag pattern down the sides.

5. Make a garland for the tree by hot-gluing rows of ½-inch cinnamon sticks, rose hips, and whole allspice between the star anise.

6. Spray the tree with the floral fixative.

7. Hot-glue the bird to one side of the tree.

Seashell Ornaments

Strolling along the seashore is one of the most refreshing ways to enjoy nature and often yields a cherished collection of seashells. These ornaments are a fun way to showcase special vacation mementos, and take just a few minutes to make.

Large Seashell Ornament

Materials

Large shell, approximately 2 × 3 inches

6 or 7 small accent shells

3 pieces of narrow satin ribbon, one 12 inches long, one 8 inches long, and one 6 inches long

Hot-glue gun and glue sticks

3-inch piece of thin-gauge wire

Wire cutters

1. Fold the 12-inch ribbon in half to form a hanging loop and hot-glue the ends to the back side of the large shell, allowing about an inch of ribbon to hang down behind the shell.

2. From the 8-inch length of ribbon, make six loops about ¾ inch high. Secure the loops together by wrapping the wire around the base of the loops and twisting it several times. Trim off any excess wire with the wire cutters and then hot-glue the loops to the top of the shell.

3. To form the streamers, hot-glue the center point of the 6-inch ribbon behind the ribbon loops on top of the shell. Hot-glue two small accent shells to each end of the streamers, one on the top side of the ribbon and another on the underside of the ribbon.

4. Hot-glue two or three accent shells around the ribbon loops on the top side of the large shell.

Seashell Cluster Ornament

Materials

3 shells, ¾ to 1 inch long

4 small accent shells

2 pieces of narrow satin ribbon, one 18 inches long and one 6 inches long

Hot-glue gun and glue sticks

1. Fold the 18-inch length of ribbon in half to make a 5-inch hanging loop with 4-inch streamers.

2. Arrange the three medium-sized shells on the ribbon at the bottom of the loop and hot-glue them in place.

3. Tie the 6-inch ribbon into a bow and hot-glue it to the center top of the shell arrangement.

4. Conceal any visible glue by hot-gluing an accent shell on the front and back sides of the shell arrangement.

5. Hot-glue an accent shell to each ribbon end.

Ribbon Ornament

Ribbons come in such an astonishing array of colors, patterns, and textures that they belong on the Christmas tree, not just on the presents underneath it. Here's a clever way to turn holiday ribbons into ornaments.

Materials

2 mountain mint leaves

4 stems of sweet Annie, 1½ inches long

2 sprigs of baby's-breath, 1½ inches long

3 stems of chamomile, 1½ inches long

1 sprig of lavender, 1½ inches long

3 sprigs of pearly everlasting, 1 inch long

4 stems of purple annual statice

1 red and yellow strawflower

5 inches of gold thread

Hot-glue gun and glue sticks

Wooden disk, 3½ inches in diameter and ¼ inch thick

7 inches of colorful holiday ribbon, at least 4 inches wide

Pencil

Scissors

10 inches of gold ribbon, ¼ inch wide

1. To make a hanger, tie the ends of the gold thread together in a loop, and hot-glue the loop to the edge of the wooden disk.

2. Lay the wooden disk on the back of the wide holiday ribbon and trace around it with the pencil. Trace around it at a second place on the ribbon and cut out both traced circles of ribbon.

3. Hot-glue the ribbon shapes to the front and back of the disk and hot-glue the narrow gold ribbon around the edge.

4. Hot-glue the two mountain mint leaves across the front of the ornament with their stems overlapping at the center.

5. Hot-glue the sweet Annie, baby's-breath, chamomile, and lavender on each side of the leaves. Hot-glue the pearly everlasting and the annual statice in place. Finally, hot-glue the strawflower in the center of the ornament, positioning it over the stems of the other materials.

Pine Needle Cross

Reminiscent of Celtic crosses, these simple ornaments are constructed of pine needles, walnut slices, and pinecone petals.

Materials

For one cross:

48 longleaf pine needle clusters, caps on

1 walnut slice, ¼ inch thick

4 pinecone petals

Large pot or heat-proof bowl

Boiling water

Towel

4 twist-ties

Brown quilting thread

Needle

Scissors

Hot-glue gun and glue sticks

Clear acrylic spray

8 inches of metallic thread

1. Put the pine needles into the pot and pour boiling water over them to cover. Allow the needles to soak for approximately 1 hour. Pour off the water and wrap the needles in a towel to keep them soft and pliable.

2. Form 12 pine needle clusters into a bundle, making sure that the ends of the caps are even. Secure the bundle with a twist-tie ½ inch below the caps. Secure the other end of the bundle with a second twist-tie about 3 inches from the end.

3. Repeat Step 2.

4. Lay the two bundles side by side, with the caps on opposite ends. Using a strong double knot, tie the two bundles together at one end with the quilting thread, just under the caps. This is now the top of the cross. Remove the twist-ties on this end of the cross.

5. For the horizontal arms of the cross, make two more bundles of 12 needle clusters each, but trim the ends without caps so that the bundles are 2 inches shorter than the vertical section of the cross. Lay the bundles side by side with the caps at opposite ends, and tie them together about 1 inch from each end.

6. Separate the needles in the vertical section just enough to be able to insert the horizontal arms through the section about 2 inches from the top. Place a twist-tie under the arms to keep them from slipping down.

7. Tie off the bottom of the vertical section with the quilting thread and trim any excess needles from the ends of the cross.

8. Check the position of the horizontal arms. Then tie a piece of quilting thread tightly around the vertical section just below and just above the arms to hold them in place.

9. Thread the needle with a piece of quilting thread and sew the nut slice to the center of the cross, making several stitches around the center of the nut membrane and through the middle of the vertical pine needles. Knot the thread on the back of the cross and trim the ends.

10. Hot-glue the four pinecone petals around the nut with the cut ends under the nut slice.

11. Spray the ornament with clear acrylic.

12. To make a hanger, form the piece of metallic thread into a loop and hot-glue it to the top of the cross on the back side.

Grass Angel Tree Topper

Wild orchard grass, free for the gathering, and hydrangea blooms make a striking angel for the top of the tree.

Materials

- 20 stalks of mature orchard grass, or other grain with mature seeds
- 2 large dried hydrangea blooms, broken into florets, 1 to 2 inches in diameter
- Pruning shears
- Tape measure or ruler
- Brown string
- Hot-glue gun and glue sticks

1. From each stalk of grass cut three pieces: one 13-inch piece that includes the seeds, and two 6-inch pieces of stem.

2. To make the body of the angel, hold the 13-inch pieces together in a bundle, aligning the seed tips as closely as possible. Measure 10 inches up from the seed tips and fold the grass stalks over at that point. Measure 1¼ inches back down from the fold and tie the stalks together with the string (see Figure 1). The side with the folded end is the back of the body.

3. To make the arms, select eight 6-inch pieces of stem. On the back of the body, insert the arms between the body and the overhang from the fold (see Figure 2). Hot-glue the arms in place.

4. To create shoulders and folded arms, bend the arms about ¾ inch out from the body, toward the front of the body. Loop the arms in a single knot. Tuck the right arm under the left and hot-glue in place.

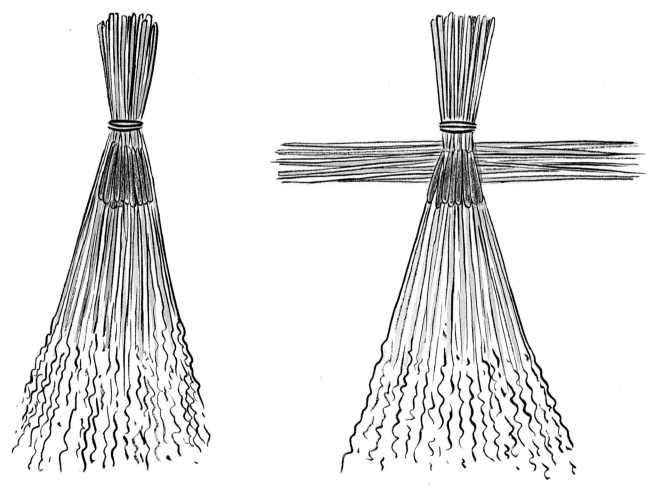

Figure 1

Figure 2

5. To make the wings, hot-glue the remaining stalks to the back in a double fan shape, working with eight stems at a time (see Figure 3).

6. Hot-glue the hydrangea florets to the ends of the wings. Hot-glue a sprig of hydrangea to the head to form a halo and in the arms to make a bouquet.

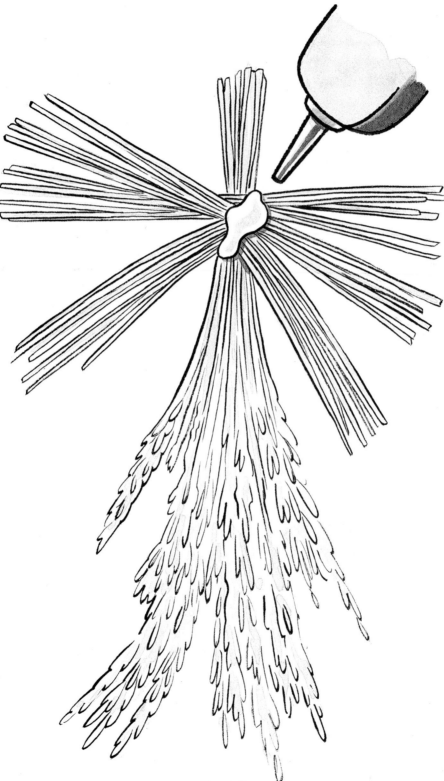

Figure 3

Downhill Racers

These jaunty skiers are ready to swoop down the slopes of your Christmas tree—or perch on a package.

Materials

For one ornament:

1 sweet gum seedpod
1 acorn with cap on
Pruning shears
2 twist-ties
Silver spray paint
Hot-glue gun and glue sticks
8 inches of heavy gold thread
8 inches of colored yarn
Black and red permanent markers with fine tips

1. Using the pruning shears, cut the stem off the sweet gum seedpod and trim the twist-ties to 2½ inches long.

2. Curl the twist-ties up slightly on one end. Spray them silver and allow them to dry.

3. Place the sweet gum seedpod on the twist-tie "skis," making sure that some of its prongs touch each ski. Hot-glue those prongs to the skis.

4. Hot-glue the acorn to the top of the sweet gum seedpod to make the head.

5. To make a hanger, tie the gold thread in a loop and hot-glue the knot to the back of the head.

6. Wrap the yarn around the neck, tie it in a knot, and trim the yarn ends to the desired length.

7. Draw the eyes with the black permanent marker and the mouth with red.

❧ The Christmas Table ❧

The groaning board, it was called in the old days, when enormous platters of food caused the old wooden tables to creak in protest. Whatever your menu, whether you choose glorious excess or sensible restraint, grace your holiday table with decorations that speak comfort and joy to all who gather there.

Lunaria Tree
and Candleholder

Lunaria, variously known as money plant, honesty, and pennies from heaven, are delicate, pearly white seedpods that are semitransparent. They add shimmering beauty to this glass candleholder and table tree.

Candleholder

Materials

    30 lunaria seedpods

    2 pieces of stick cinnamon, 1½ inches long

    2 star anise

    Hot-glue gun and glue sticks

    2-inch-diameter glass votive candleholder, 3 inches high

    16 inches of cream ribbon with gold edges, ⅛ inch wide

    Scissors

    White votive candle

1. Peel off the outer covering from the lunaria seedpods and remove the seeds.

2. Hot-glue a row of lunaria around the top of the glass candleholder, overlapping the sides of the lunaria and allowing the top one-third of each one to project above the rim of the glass.

3. Hot-glue additional rows of lunaria to the glass, making sure that each row overlaps the previous one.

4. Wrap the ribbon around the votive glass and tie it in a knot. Trim the ends to 1 inch.

5. Hot-glue the two pieces of cinnamon stick horizontally, above and below the ribbon knot.

6. Hot-glue a star anise on top of the knot. Break the other star anise in half. Hot-glue one half to the upper cinnamon piece and the other half to the lower cinnamon piece.

7. Place the candle inside. When the candle is lit, be sure the flame is not near the exposed lunaria edges at the top of the glass. Never leave a lit candle unattended.

Table Tree

Materials

    156 lunaria seedpods

    12 star anise

    Hot-glue gun and glue sticks

    12-inch foam cone

    5-inch-diameter metal stand, 3 inches high

1. Hot-glue the foam cone to the metal stand.

2. Peel off the outer covering from the lunaria seedpods and remove the seeds.

3. Hot-glue a row of lunaria around the base of the cone, overlapping the sides of the lunaria. Working from bottom to top, add additional rows until the cone is covered, making sure that each row overlaps the previous one.

4. Hot-glue one star anise at the top of the tree and space the others randomly around the tree.

Garlic Wreath

With its round, knobby shape and thin, papery skin, garlic is an interesting-looking herb. This culinary wreath displays it to advantage and makes a great gift for a cook. Decorative "flowers" of bay leaves and cressia pods add touches of color.

Materials

15 to 20 whole heads of garlic
20 large bay leaves
8 cressia pods
22 to 30 small bay leaves
10 tiny seedheads from grasses
10-inch piece of heavy-gauge floral wire
14-inch-diameter, bleached-rattan wreath base
3 yards of raffia
Hot-glue gun and glue sticks

1. Make a hanger for the wreath by wrapping one end of the heavy-gauge wire around a section of rattan on the back side of the wreath base and bending the other end of the wire into a loop. (See "Making Hangers" on page 22.)

2. Fill the wreath base with the garlic heads. If necessary, gently separate the pieces of rattan in order to force the larger heads into the base.

3. Using the raffia, tie any loose, unstable garlic heads onto the back side of the wreath.

4. To make each large "flower," hot-glue ten large bay leaves in a circle. Hot-glue two cressia pods to the center, then hot-glue seven or eight small bay leaves around the pods for a three-dimensional effect. Hot-glue five grass seedheads around the center of the flower to resemble stamens.

5. To make each small flower, glue four to seven small bay leaves in a half circle, then glue two cressia pods over the bases of the leaves.

Raffia Napkin Ring

This braided-raffia ring adds a distinctive accent to your holiday table with its colorful dried fruit and angular star anise.

Materials

Dried orange slice, 1½ inches in diameter (See "Drying Fruit" on page 28.)

Dried apple slice, 1½ inches in diameter

Star anise

28 strands of raffia, 15 inches long

Twist-tie

Scissors

Hot-glue gun and glue sticks

1. Form 27 strands of the raffia into one bunch, and secure one end of the bunch with a twist-tie (see Figure 1).

2. Divide the bunched strands into three groups of nine, and braid them. Cut off the untied end to make a 12-inch-long braid.

3. Form the braid into a circle about 3 inches in diameter, allowing the ends to overlap. Use the remaining strand of raffia to tie the braid together where the ends cross, wrapping the raffia around the braid three times and making a double knot (see Figure 2). Trim the ends of the raffia tie.

4. Remove the twist-tie, fluff both ends of the braid, and trim the ends to about 1 inch.

5. Hot-glue the orange slice to the braid, covering the raffia knot. Glue the apple slice to the orange and the star anise to the apple.

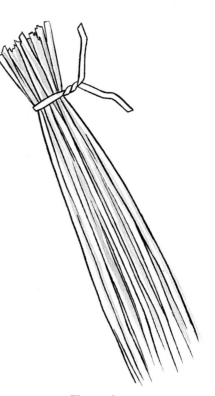

Figure 1

Figure 2

Juniper Berry
Mini Wreaths

These blue and silver wreaths make perfect candle rings for your holiday table. Each one can be made to fit whatever size candle you choose to encircle.

Materials

For one wreath:

10 stems of 'Silver King' artemisia, four
      6 inches long and six 3 inches long

6 sprigs of juniper foliage and berries,
      2 inches long

Wire cutters or heavy-duty scissors

Heavy-gauge floral wire

Candle

Monofilament fishing line

Hot-glue gun and glue sticks

1. To make the base for the candle ring, cut a piece of wire long enough to work with—say, 12 inches—and bend it around the candle you plan to use. Twist the ends of the wire together to hold the ring shape and remove the candle. Trim any wire ends.

2. Working with two 6-inch stems of artemisia at a time, position them against the wire base and twist them around it, overlapping as necessary. Secure the artemisia to the base by wrapping it tightly with monofilament at ½-inch intervals. Repeat this process until the base is covered.

3. Hot-glue the 3-inch sprigs of artemisia evenly around the wreath base and hot-glue the sprigs of juniper to the artemisia.

4. Be sure your candle is tall enough to clear the greenery and never leave a lit candle unattended.

This festive holiday table sports a Victorian tree ornament (see page 188), a decorated package (see page 200), a rustic basket with wheat (see page 232), a bay leaf flower (see page 237), and a table garland (see page 245).

Rustic Basket with Wheat

A rustic basket decorated with wheat, ribbons, and evergreens makes a fine arrangement just as it is, or it can be a handsome container for potpourri, walnuts, or small apples.

Materials

50 stalks of wheat, 18 inches long

10 twigs, ¼ inch in diameter and 9 inches long

2 stems of red-dyed sorghum

2 dried apple slices

8 stems of Fraser fir, 4 to 5 inches long

10 × 5 × 3-inch birch-bark basket with handle

Medium-gauge floral wire

Wire cutters

Heavy-duty scissors

1½ yards of plaid ribbon, 1 inch wide

6 yards of red raffia

Hot-glue gun and glue sticks

1. Arrange the wheat in a bundle so that the heads fan out slightly in an attractive shape. Lay the bundle in the basket, positioning it toward the back of the basket and centered from side to side so that the ends project from the sides of the basket an equal distance. Wire the wheat securely to the handle. Trim any stray stalk ends so that the stems are fairly even.

2. Form the twigs into a bundle and wire them to the handle at the front of the basket, positioning them on the outside of the basket.

3. Cut off an 18-inch length of ribbon and cut it down the middle lengthwise to make a piece ½ inch wide. Tie it into a bow and wire it at its center. Using the remaining 1-inch-wide ribbon, make a six-loop bow and wire it together. Form the raffia into a bow, leaving four streamers 18 inches long. (See "Making Bows" on page 30.)

4. Wire the large ribbon bow to the wheat bundle and the raffia bow to the ribbon bow. Wire the small ribbon bow to the handle on the front of the basket. Bring the long streamers from the raffia bow across the basket and thread the ends through the loops of the small ribbon bow.

5. Hot-glue the sorghum, dried apple slices, and fir sprigs around each bow.

Hornets' Nest Centerpiece

Hornets' nests, which are often abandoned in the winter and then fall to the ground from tree branches, are tempting materials for nature crafters. To ensure that the warmth of your home does not encourage larvae to mature and emerge, you'll need to follow several safety precautions. First, watch the nest carefully to make sure it's abandoned. (Looks can be deceiving, though, since hornets build their nests in layers; it's quite possible that the outer layers could be empty while a brood of hornets lies in one of the underlayers.) Then put the nest in a large plastic freezer bag and place it in a freezer that is reliably 0˚F or colder for two weeks.

Materials

4 pinecones, 1 inch long

Hornets' nest

3 crabapple branches, 12 inches long

9 stems of ivy, 14 inches long

8 red carnations

5 chestnuts

3 small clumps of garden moss

Hot-glue gun and glue sticks

4 × 5-inch block of wet floral foam

Plastic sheeting

Floral tape

1. Bake the pinecones at 200°F for 25 minutes to kill any insect eggs or larvae.

2. Tear open the top of the hornets' nest, remove the hive, and turn the nest upside down.

3. Place two of the crabapple branches on top of the nest with their stems facing each other at about the center point of the nest. Hot-glue them in place, then hot-glue the remaining crabapple branch with its cut stem facing the cut stems of the previous two.

4. Turn the nest right side up and hot-glue the hive against one side of the nest, using the photo as a positioning guide.

5. Place the floral foam on top of the plastic and fold the plastic about ¾ inch up the sides of the foam. Secure the plastic in place with floral tape, then carefully place the foam inside the hornets' nest.

6. Gently insert all of the ivy stems into the foam. Next, loosely wrap the protruding ivy stems around the crabapple branches. Arrange several carnations in a cluster inside the hornets' nest and hot-glue them in place.

7. Finish by hot-gluing the chestnuts, cones, and moss onto the crabapple branches in a random fashion.

Variation: If you like the bright colors and whimsical style of this project, but haven't stumbled upon an abandoned hornets' nest lately, you might consider the wreath centerpiece shown below. Begin by covering the foam with plastic as you did for the hornets' nest arrangement. Wire the plastic-covered foam to one of the inside edges of a vine wreath base. Place three ivy stems aside and then insert the remaining ivy and the carnations into the foam to form a triangular shape. Weave some of the longer ivy stems around the sides of the wreath base. Cut each of the reserved ivy stems into three or four shorter lengths, and then arrange them strategically to cover any visible foam. To finish, fold a 3-yard length of ¹⁄₁₆-inch satin ribbon in half and loosely weave it around the wreath base, securing occasionally with hot glue as needed.

Bay Leaf Flower

Welcome your dinner guests with bay leaves, one of the oldest and most beloved of herbs. For each guest, sketch a simple bay leaf design on a plain place card and make a bay leaf "flower" to complete the place setting.

Materials

8 large bay leaves

2 to 3 cressia pods

6 small bay leaves

4 to 6 seedheads of tiny grasses

Hot-glue gun and glue sticks

1½-inch-diameter circle of heavy paper

1. Hot-glue the large bay leaves around the paper circle, allowing the ends to project over the edge.

2. Hot-glue the cressia pods into the center of the circle and the small bay leaves around the pods.

3. Finally, create stamens for the flower by hot-gluing the grass seedheads under the pods.

Variation: To turn the bay leaf flower into a Christmas tree ornament, use poster board or other lightweight cardboard for the backing. Make a hanger by folding an 8-inch piece of raffia in half and hot-gluing the ends to the back of the cardboard.

Culinary Wreath

As decorative as they are flavorful, herbs are welcome additions to the Christmas table. Bay and sage, oregano and thyme add their fragrant foliage to this culinary wreath.

Materials

40 stems of 'Silver King' artemisia, ten 24 inches long and thirty 4 inches long

24 bay leaves

1 stem of pepperberries

15 chive blossoms

1 sprig of thyme, 2 inches in diameter

2 clusters of tansy flowers, 2 inches in diameter

1 small stem of sweet Annie

1 stem of 'Silver Mound' artemisia, 3 inches long

4 garlic blossoms

2 stems of lamb's-ears

4 bee balm flowers, 3 inches in diameter

2 yarrow blooms, 2 inches in diameter

12 red chili peppers, 1½ inches long

2 small bunches of oregano

2 or 3 sprigs of sage

15 lavender flowers

3 anise hyssop flowers

8-inch single wire wreath base

Monofilament fishing line

Hot-glue gun and glue sticks

1 yard of green patterned ribbon, 1 inch wide

Floral pick

1. Working with two 24-inch stems of 'Silver King' artemisia at a time, position them against the wire wreath base and twist them around it, overlapping as necessary. Secure the artemisia to the base by wrapping it tightly with monofilament fishing line in 2-inch intervals. Repeat this process until the base is covered.

2. Hot-glue the 4-inch pieces of artemisia around the wreath, with some of the feathery foliage to the outside of the wreath and some to the inside.

3. Hot-glue the herbs and flowers to the base, distributing them evenly around the wreath.

4. Make a bow with 16-inch streamers from the green ribbon (see "Making Bows" on page 30) and wire it to a floral pick. Insert the pick into the top of the wreath in back, allowing a few of the bow's loops to show through and the streamers to hang below the wreath.

Candle Rings

Candles brighten the room and lift the spirits. These festive boxwood
rings turn simple red tapers into graceful Christmas table decorations.

Materials

8 hemlock cones, or other small cones

1 small branch of boxwood

1 stem of baby's-breath

1 stem of artemisia

Polyurethane spray

Serrated knife or coping saw

2 × 3 × 4-inch piece of floral foam

2 candles, 8 to 12 inches tall

Pencil or pen

4 yards of red ribbon, $\frac{3}{16}$-inch wide

1 yard of fine-gauge floral wire

Wire cutters or heavy-duty scissors

Hot-glue gun and glue sticks

1 floral pick

2 candleholders, wide enough to hold
   3-inch-diameter candles (optional)

1. Bake the hemlock cones at 200°F for 25 minutes to kill any insect eggs or larvae. Allow them to cool, then spray them with polyurethane.

2. With the serrated knife or coping saw, cut the foam into two layers, so that you have two 3-inch by 4-inch pieces about 1 inch thick. Cut each piece into a circle 2½ inches in diameter.

3. Stand a candle in the center of one circle and trace around the bottom of the candle with the pen or pencil. Repeat on the other foam circle. Using the knife or saw, cut out the hole you have traced.

4. Make four 3-inch-diameter ribbon bows (see "Making Bows" on page 30), using 1 yard of ribbon for each bow. Leave 5- to 6-inch-long streamers, trimming the ends on the diagonal. As you finish each bow, secure it with wire. Trim the wire ends to ¼ inch with the wire cutters or heavy-duty scissors.

5. Position two bows opposite each other on each foam ring. Secure by placing hot glue on the wire ends and inserting them into the foam.

6. Cut the boxwood, baby's-breath, and artemisia into small pieces.

7. Beginning with the boxwood, place hot glue on the stem end of each piece, and insert it into the foam ring. Try to keep the arrangement open and airy. If necessary, use the pointed end of the floral pick to help hold the material in place until the glue dries and hardens.

8. Glue the hemlock cones evenly around the wreath, and fill in with more baby's-breath and artemisia if necessary.

9. The candle rings can be set directly on the table as freestanding decorations. If desired, place the arrangements on purchased candleholders.

Moss Table Decorations

The green of garden moss, the rich red of rose hips and ornamental peppers, an occasional touch of gold metallic ribbon—the combination is repeated in a tiny topiary, a miniature tree for the Christmas table, and a napkin ring for each guest.

Tiny Topiary

Materials

- 12-inch-square clump of garden moss
- 15 rose hips
- 12 red ornamental peppers, ½ inch long
- Hot-glue gun and glue sticks
- 2 foam balls, 2 inches in diameter
- 2½-inch-diameter clay flowerpot, 2 inches high
- ¼-inch-diameter wooden dowel, 6 inches long
- Pruning shears
- Floral pins
- Floral fixative spray
- 30 inches of metallic gold ribbon, ½ inch wide, cut into one 10-inch piece and one 20-inch piece
- Scissors

1. Hot-glue a foam ball into the opening of the clay flowerpot.

2. Push the dowel about halfway into the center of the foam ball.

3. Take the other foam ball and push it onto the top of the dowel.

4. Using the shears, cut the moss into pieces of manageable size and attach them to the foam balls with floral pins, covering all visible foam completely.

5. Hot-glue the rose hips over the tops of the floral pins to conceal them, then hot-glue the ornamental peppers to the moss in a random pattern.

6. Spray the topiary with floral fixative.

7. Wrap the 10-inch piece of the gold ribbon around the flowerpot, positioning it low in back and crossing it near the rim in front. Hot-glue the ribbon in place and trim the ends on the diagonal.

8. Make a bow (see "Making Bows" on page 30) with the remaining ribbon and hot-glue it to the crossed ribbon on the flowerpot.

Table Tree

Materials

- 13 × 20-inch clump of garden moss
- 16 rose hips
- 35 red ornamental peppers, ½ to 1 inch long
- Hot-glue gun and glue sticks
- 12-inch foam cone
- 6-inch-diameter metal stand, 3 inches high
- Pruning shears
- Floral pins
- Floral fixative spray

1. Hot-glue the foam cone to the stand.

2. Using the shears, cut the moss into pieces of manageable size and wrap them around the cone, covering it completely. Secure the moss with floral pins.

3. Hot-glue the rose hips over the tops of the floral pins to conceal them.

4. Hot-glue the peppers to the moss in a random pattern.

5. Spray the tree with floral fixative.

Napkin Ring

Materials

- 2-inch clump of garden moss
- 1 rose hip
- 2 red ornamental peppers, ½ inch long
- Hot-glue gun and glue sticks
- 2-inch-diameter vine wreath base
- 2 inches of gold metallic ribbon, ½ inch wide
- 2-inch piece of fine-gauge floral wire
- Heavy-duty scissors

1. Using your hands, separate the clump of moss into strands. Select the best-looking strands and hot-glue them around the outside of the vine wreath base.

2. Tie the metallic ribbon in the center of the moss to form a simple bow. Wire it around the middle to hold it and trim the wire ends with the scissors.

3. Hot-glue the rose hip over the wire on the bow, then hot-glue the peppers on each side of the bow.

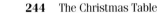

Table Garland and Chair Swag

Whether you plan an intimate Christmas supper for 2 or a lavish banquet for 20, a fresh evergreen garland draped around the table will make the occasion memorable. A festive bow can be placed at each corner, at the top of each drape, or both. A matching chair swag ties it all together.

Garland

Materials

For each 3-foot section of garland:

2 medium pinecones

32 stems of freshly cut white pine, 12 inches long

8 stems of freshly cut hemlock, 12 inches long

8 sprigs of freshly cut holly, 6 inches long

2 stems of caspia, 6 inches long

2 sprigs of canella berries

2 red chili peppers

2 garlic bulbs

2 Chinese lanterns

Tape measure or yardstick

Heavy-gauge floral wire

Wire cutters

Hot-glue gun and glue sticks

1½ yards of wired ribbon, 3 inches wide, for each bow

Floral tape or masking tape

1. Bake the pinecones at 200°F for 25 minutes to kill any insect eggs or larvae.

2. With the tape measure or yardstick, measure the circumference of your table. You will need a garland twice that long in order for it to drape in graceful curves. If you divide the total desired length by three, you'll know how many 3-foot lengths of garland to make.

3. Take the pine greens and make eight mini bunches of three stems per bunch. Make eight more bunches of mixed greens: one stem of pine, one stem of hemlock, and one sprig of holly. To form the garland's base, wire the evergreen groups to each other securely end to end, alternating the pine bundles with the mixed ones. Take care that the greens of each new bouquet cover the stems of the previous bouquet and that all of the stems face in the same direction.

4. Wire the caspia and canella berries evenly along the garland, positioning them so that their stems are wired over the wired stems of the greenery.

5. Hot-glue the peppers, garlic bulbs, Chinese lanterns, and pinecones to the greenery, spacing them evenly along the garland.

6. Make a bow with 2-foot streamers from the wired ribbon and wire it to the garland. (See "Making Bows" on page 30.)

7. If you plan to attach the garland to an older table or one held together with screws or pegs, there will probably be gaps between the top of the leg and the bottom of the tabletop. Cut 12-inch lengths of floral wire and wrap them with floral tape, to avoid scratching the table. Wrap the taped wire around the garland and then around the joint of leg and tabletop. If there are no points of purchase for wiring, tape the garland to the table legs with masking tape or other easily removable tape, taking care to conceal the tape in the foliage.

Chair Swag

Materials

3 medium pinecones

10 stems of freshly cut hemlock, seven 3 feet long and three 1 foot long

4 stems of caspia, three 12 inches long and one 8 inches long

1 sprig of canella berries

Heavy- and medium-gauge floral wire

Wire cutters

Hot-glue gun and glue sticks

1½ yards of wired ribbon, 3 inches wide

1. Bake the pinecones at 200°F for 25 minutes to kill any insect eggs or larvae.

2. Arrange the seven long stems of hemlock and the three long stems of caspia in a fan shape with the caspia on top. Wire the stems together with the heavy-gauge wire about 3 inches from the ends of their stems.

3. Arrange the remaining evergreens and caspia in a second bouquet, center it on top of the first, and secure the two with heavy-gauge floral wire, making a loop for hanging.

4. Using the medium-gauge wire, wire the three cones together at their bases. (See "Floral Wire" on page 17.) Slip the wire ends through the wire around the bouquets and twist to secure.

5. Slip the stem of the canella berries under the heavy-gauge floral wire, reinforcing with a dab of hot glue if needed.

6. Form a large bow from the ribbon, wiring the bow around its center and twisting the wire ends around the stems of the bouquet, covering any visible wire. (See "Making Bows" on page 30.)

Candle Wreaths

Purchased miniature wreaths make quick and easy bases for natural materials. Choose a wreath base made of greens, vine, or straw and hot-glue berries and dried flowers around each one to create these elegant, red and white candleholders for your Christmas table.

Pepperberry Candle Wreath

Materials

    25 sprigs of German statice, 1 inch long

    2 to 4 clusters of pepperberries

    Hot-glue gun and glue sticks

    3-inch-diameter wreath base

1. Hot-glue the German statice in a spiral pattern around the wreath base, covering the top and sides.

2. Hot-glue the pepperberries to the German statice, encircling the top of the wreath.

Floral Candle Wreath

Materials

    15 sprigs of German statice, 1 inch long

    3-inch-diameter cockscomb bloom, cut into three ½-inch clusters

    1 stem of white statice, cut into ten ½-inch pieces

    1 sprig of pearly everlasting, cut into three ½-inch pieces

    3 white strawflowers

    1 stem of pepperberries, cut into three ½-inch clusters

    Hot-glue gun and glue sticks

    3-inch-diameter wreath base

1. Hot-glue the German statice in a spiral pattern around the wreath base, covering the top and sides.

2. Hot-glue the other flowers and the pepperberries to the German statice, distributing the materials evenly around the wreath.

Branch Centerpiece

This eye-catching centerpiece uses several branch-es as a base. Although the nesting bird makes a fun focal point for this arrangement, feel free to use a cherished family ornament instead.

Materials

3 interesting branches, 14 to 16 inches long and about 2 inches in diameter

17 stems of eucalyptus, six 12 inches long, five 7 inches long, and six 3 inches long

14 straws of oats or rye, seven 17 inches long and seven 8 inches long

8 small clumps of garden moss

6 dried pomegranates, 4 whole and 2 broken

10 stems of silk heather, five 6 inches long and four 4 inches long

18- to 24-inch stem of silk blackberries, cut into 3-inch pieces

8 clumps of pepperberries, 2 large, 2 medium, and 4 small

3 pieces of medium-gauge floral wire, one 18 inches long and two 5 inches long

Hot-glue gun and glue sticks

Wire cutters

Small artificial bird, 2½ inches from beak to tail

1. Arrange the branches over each other in a crisscross pattern. Secure them together with the 18-inch piece of floral wire and then reinforce with hot glue. Trim off any excess wire with the wire cutters.

2. Insert the 12- and 7-inch eucalyptus stems under the branches and hot-glue in place, taking care to space them fairly evenly.

3. Bundle the 8-inch oat straws, wiring the bundle together about 1 inch from the ends. Repeat with the 17-inch oat straws.

4. Arrange one oat bundle on each side of the branches near the eucalyptus and hot-glue in place.

5. Create a small nest shape from one of the moss clusters and hot-glue it to the top of the arrangement, then glue in the bird.

6. Cluster the pomegranates around the nest and hot-glue them in place. (Tip: To crack a pomegranate, insert the tip of a steak knife about ¼ inch through the shell and twist the knife gently. A piece will crack and split off.)

7. Hot-glue the heather stems around the nest, allowing their natural curves to form around the nest. Fill in any space around the nest with the 3-inch eucalyptus stems and the silk blackberry pieces.

8. Hot-glue a large clump of pepperberries near the oats and eucalyptus on each side, then arrange the remaining pepperberry clusters around the arrangement and hot-glue them in place.

9. Finish by covering any visible gaps or floral wire with the remaining clumps of moss.

Mail-Order Sources

Capriland's Herb Farm
534 Silver Street
North Coventry, CT 06238
Offers flowers and herbs.

Prim Pines
2463 Farm Life School Road
Carthage, NC 28327
Offers nut slices and pine needles.
Send stamped, self-addressed envelope
for price list.

Rasland Farm
N.C. 82 at U.S. 13
Godwin, NC 28344
Offers flowers and herbs.

The Sassafrass Hutch
11880 Sandy Bottom, NE
Greenville, MI 48838
Offers flowers and herbs.

Sinking Springs Herb Farm
234 Blair Shore Road
Elkton, MD 21921
Offers flowers and herbs.

Smile Herb Shop
4908 Berwyn Road
College Park, MD 20740
Offers flowers and herbs.

Stillridge Herb Farm
10370 Route 99
Woodstock, MD 21163
Offers flowers and herbs.

Tom Thumb Workshops
P.O. Box 322
Chincoteague, VA 23336
Offers flowers and herbs.

Well-Sweep Herb Farm
317 Mount Bethel Road
Port Murray, NJ 07865
Offers flowers and herbs.

Bibliography

Brady, Sally Ryder. *A Yankee Christmas.* Emmaus, Pa.: Yankee Books, 1992.

Carlson, Eric. *The Holiday Wreath Book.* New York: Sterling Publishing Co., 1992.

Carlson, Eric, Dawn Cusick, and Carol Taylor. *The Complete Book of Nature Crafts.* Emmaus, Pa.: Rodale Press, 1992.

Christmas at Home. Des Moines, Iowa: Better Homes and Gardens Books, 1992.

Cusick, Dawn. *Potpourri Crafts.* New York: Sterling Publishing Co., 1992.

———. *A Scented Christmas.* New York: Sterling Publishing Co., 1991.

———. *Wreath-Making Basics.* New York: Sterling Publishing Co., 1993.

Holiday Welcome Wreaths. Emmaus, Pa.: Rodale Press, 1993.

LaRose-Weaver, Diane, and Dawn Cusick. *A Fireside Christmas.* New York: Sterling Publishing Co., 1992.

Mallow, Judy. *Pine Needle and Nut Crafting.* Carthage, N.C.: Judy Mallow, 1984.

Platt, Ellen Spector. *Flower Crafts.* Emmaus, Pa.: Rodale Press, 1993.

———. *Wreaths, Arrangements, and Basket Decorations.* Emmaus, Pa.: Rodale Press, 1994.

Prawat, Carolyn Mordecai. *Gourd Craft.* Mount Gilead, Ohio: American Gourd Society, 1978.

Pulleyn, Rob. *The Wreath Book.* New York: Sterling Publishing Co., 1988.

Taylor, Carol. *Christmas Naturals.* New York: Sterling Publishing Co., 1991.

———. *Herbal Wreaths.* New York: Sterling Publishing Co., 1992.

———. *Treasures for the Christmas Tree: 101 Festive Ornaments to Make and Enjoy.* New York: Sterling Publishing Co., 1994.

INDEX

By Subject

A

Accent materials, attaching, 25

Angels, 36, 140, 218

Artemisia, projects using, 60, 107, 229, 238

B

Background materials, attaching, 24

Bases
  basic instructions, 19–21
  curved, 20
  double-wire, 20–21
  foam, 19
  grapevine wreath, 20
  herbal, 21
  single-wire, 20
  straw, 21
  twig, 19–20
  vine, 19–20
  wire, 20–21

Baskets, 52, 156, 232

Bay leaves, projects using, 120, 169, 173, 212, 227, 237, 238

Berries, projects using
  canella, 58, 73, 76, 245, 246
  other, 84, 229
  pepperberries, 39, 82, 88, 106, 108, 110, 112, 114, 124, 134, 248, 250

Birch bark, project using, 147

Birch log, project using, 126

Birds, artificial, projects using, 114, 153, 156, 177, 205, 212, 250

Bows, making, 30–31

Boxwood, projects using, 52, 58, 82, 84, 88, 110, 124, 126, 202, 207, 240

C

Candles, projects using, 84, 224, 240, 244, 250

Caspia, projects using, 73, 76, 86, 147, 152, 165, 245, 246

Cedar, projects using, 42, 44, 58, 92, 110, 124, 165, 170

Centerpieces, 84, 107, 126, 224, 234, 244, 250

Cinnamon sticks, projects using, 107, 112, 139, 152, 166, 173, 202, 207, 208, 212, 224

Cool-glue guns, 18

Cones, projects using, 77, 86, 97, 101, 120, 156, 183, 188, 198, 203, 240. *See also* Pinecones

Cord, jute, 25

Cornhusks, project using, 164

Creche, 136

D

Driftwood, projects using, 102, 186

E

Eggs, project using, 160

Eucalyptus, projects using, 97, 250

Evergreens, projects using, 92, 101, 106, 139, 147, 232, 245, 246

F

Ferns, projects using, 44, 52, 60, 88, 112, 114, 126, 129, 171, 183, 198, 202

Fir, Fraser, projects using, 42, 45, 52, 112, 117, 202, 232

Floral foam, fine-grained, 26, 28 "wet," 26

Floral picks, 16

Floral pins, 17

Floral tape, 17

Floral wire, 17–18

Flowers
  drying of, 27–28
  handling of, 26, 28
  projects using, 82, 94, 98, 101, 108, 110, 117, 120, 124, 134, 136, 152, 166, 169, 170, 173, 197, 202, 204, 215, 238, 248

Fruit
  drying, 28–29
  projects using, 101, 166, 173, 189, 208, 232

Fungi, project using, 153

G

Garlands, 58, 120, 175, 245
  basic instructions, 25–26

Garlic, projects using, 58, 227, 245

Gift-wrap decorations, 44, 86, 200, 212

Glue, white craft, 19

Gourds
  hard-shell, 29
  projects using, 54, 89, 121,

131, 190, 191
  seasoning, 29
  using, 29

Grapevines, projects using, 58, 82, 143, 147

Grasses, wild, projects using, 218, 227, 237

H

Hangers
  foam-backed swag, 23
  making, 22–23
  vertical swag, 23
  wreath, 22

Herbs
  drying, 27–28
  handling, 26, 28
  projects using, 94, 101, 107, 117, 120, 136, 138, 139, 169, 173, 188, 203, 212, 215, 227, 237, 238

Hornets' nest, project using, 234

Horns, projects using, 97, 169

Hot-glue guns, 18

Hydrangea blooms, project using, 218

J

Juniper, projects using, 84, 229

L

Lotus pods, project using, 36

Lunaria seedpods, projects using, 108, 120, 188, 224

M

Magnolia leaves, project using, 144

Milkweed pod, project using, 205

Mini bouquets, 16

Monofilament fishing line, 18

Moss
  garden, projects using, 82, 108, 117, 136, 177, 204, 232, 242, 244, 250
  Spanish, projects using, 61, 112, 114, 124, 126, 150, 156, 200

O

Okra, project using, 185

Ornaments, 64, 149–221

P

Peppers, ornamental, projects using, 242, 244, 245

Pine, white, projects using, 58, 73, 76, 152, 170, 245

Pinecones, projects using, 44, 45, 52, 60, 69, 73, 76, 77, 92, 147, 150, 153, 159, 202, 245, 246

Pine needles
crafting with, 29–30
loblolly, 30
longleaf, 30
ponderosa, 30
projects using, 48, 101, 140, 156, 177, 183, 197, 209, 217
slash, 30

Pomanders, 189, 203

Pomegranates, projects using, 36, 147, 173, 250

Potpourri
projects using, 96, 117, 134
recipes, 101

R

Rose hips, projects using, 101, 139, 188, 242, 244

Roses, projects using, 82, 88, 96, 101, 112, 117, 124, 126, 166, 173

S

Sachets, 134

Santas, 54, 102, 185, 192

Seashells, projects using, 214

Seedpods, projects using, 78, 108, 129, 140, 159, 171, 186, 203, 221, 224, 227, 237. *See also* Lunaria seedpods

Silica gel, 28

Simmers, 138, 139

Soaps, 86

Statice, projects using, 42, 45, 69, 78, 92, 94, 96, 110, 124, 126, 152, 170, 178, 203, 248

Swags, 26, 38, 44, 45, 60, 69, 73, 76, 92, 110, 143, 245
horizontal, 26

T

Tools, selecting, 16–19

Topiaries, 82, 112, 242

Tree toppers, 164, 166, 218

Tussie mussies, 106, 188

Twigs, projects using, 42, 114, 153, 232, 250

W

Walnuts, projects using, 92, 156, 175, 196, 206, 217

Wheat, projects using, 38, 232

Wreaths, 36, 42, 48, 73, 77, 124, 129, 147, 171, 227, 238
basic instructions, 24–25
mini, 171, 229, 248

By Project Title

A

Artemisia Crescent, 60

B

Baby in a Cradle, 192

Bay Leaf Flower, 237

Bay Tree Package, 212

Birch Log Arrangement, 126

Birdhouses, 114, 204

Bird Roosts, 204

Birdseed Ornaments, 64

Black Walnut Garland, 175

Blooming Candle, 84

Blown Glass Ornaments, 170

Braided Pine Needle Wreath, 48

Braided Pine Ornaments, 183

Braided Raffia Swag, 45

Branch Centerpiece, 250

C

Candleholder, 224

Candle Rings, 240

Candle Wreaths, 248

Cedar and Pepperberry Swag, 110

Cedar Swag, 44

Chair Swag, 246

Christmas Horn, 97

Christmas Simmers, 138

Cinnamon-Orange Stick, 208

Cinnamon Stick Ornaments, 207

Cinnamon Sticks, 202

Citrus Spice Simmer, 138

Cornhusk Tree Topper, 164

Cowboy Christmas, 202

Creche with Christmas Herbs, 136

Culinary Wreath, 238

D

Decorated Pomegranate, 173

Decorated Sachets, 134

Door Wreath, 73

Downhill Racers, 221

Driftwood Santas, 102

E

Elf, 194

Evergreen and Birch Bark Wreath, 147

Evergreen Herb Simmer, 139

Evergreen Potpourri, 101

Evergreen Swag, 92

F

Fabulous Fruit Ornaments, 173

Floral Bouquet Tree Topper, 166

Floral Candle Wreath, 248

Floral Horns, 169

Floral Potpourri, 101

Flower and Leaf Garland, 120

Found Ornaments, 186

Fragrant Tussie Mussie, 106

G

Garland, 245

Garlic Wreath, 227

Gift Cards, 152

Gift-Wrapped Glycerin Soaps, 86

Gourd Christmas Tree, 121

Gourd Ornaments, 191

Gourd Wise Men, 130

Grass Angel Tree Topper, 218

Green Soap with Red Ribbon, 86

Guest Room Decorations, 112

H

Hanging Holiday Basket, 51

Hornets' Nest Centerpiece, 234

Hot-Air Balloon, 190

J

Juniper Berry Mini Wreaths, 229

K

Kissing Ball, 108

L

Lamp Swag, 76

Lotus Pod and Pomegranate Wreath, 36

Lunaria Tree and Candleholder, 224

M

Magnolia Swag, 143

Maple Pod Wreath, 129

Mice in a Nutshell, 206

Milkweed Pod Ornament, 205

Moss Table Decorations, 242

Moss Tree, 107

N

Napkin Ring, 244

O

Okra Ornament, 185

Orange and Bay Leaf Ornament, 173

Owl Ornaments, 196

P

Package Decorations, 200

Painted Eggs, 160

Pepperberry Candle Wreath, 248

Pinecone Angels, 140

Pinecone Bird Nest, 150

Pinecone Swag, 69

Pinecone Wreath, 77

Pine Needle Basket, 156

Pine Needle Birdcage, 177

Pine Needle Broom Ornament, 197

Pine Needle Cross, 217

Pine Needle Doll Ornament, 209

Pink Foil Package, 94

Pink Soap with Lacy Ribbon, 77

Pomander Ornament, 189

Potpourri Jar, 117

Potpourris, 101

Purple Soap, 88

R

Raffia and Red Flowers, 202

Raffia Napkin Ring, 227

Red and White Floral Wreath, 124

Red Striped Package, 94

Ribbon Ornament, 215

Rosemary Bath Fragrance, 117

Rose Topiary, 82

Rustic Basket with Wheat, 232

S

Santa, 192

Santa Greeting Gourds, 54

Scented Bath Decorations, 117

Seashell Cluster Ornaments, 214

Seashell Ornaments, 214

Spicy Hanging Pomander, 203

Spiral Garland, 58

Stuffed Stocking and Package Decorations, 94

Sweet Gum Candy Canes, 159

Sweet Gum Mini Wreath, 171

T

Table Garland and Chair Swag, 245

Table Trees, 224, 244

Tiny Topiaries, 82, 242

Topiaries, 82, 112

Tussie Mussie Ornament, 188

Twig Ornament, 153

Twig Wreath, 42

V

Victorian Tree Ornaments, 188

W

Wheat Swag, 38

White Pine Decorations, 73

Wood-Burned Gourd, 89